THE BIG 5-INGREDIENT SIMPLE COOKBOOK

THE BIG 5-INGREDIENT SIMPLE COOKBOOK

150 SUPER EASY RECIPES

KAREN LEE YOUNG

ROCKRIDGE PRESS

For general information on our other products and services or to obtain technical support, please contact our Customer Care Department within the United States at (866) 744-2665, or outside the United States at (510) 253-0500.

Rockridge Press publishes its books in a variety of electronic and print formats. Some content that appears in print may not be available in electronic books, and vice versa.

Interior and Cover Designer: Carlos Esparza
Art Producer: Maya Melenchuk
Editor: Anna Pulley
Production Editor: Ashley Polikoff

Cover: Orecchiette with Broccoli Rabe and Sausage, page 74

Photography © 2022 Laura Flippen, cover, p. 10; © Evi Abeler pp. 53, 202; © Johnny Autry pp. 48–49; © Hélène DuJardin, pp. 42, 83, 122, 139, 149, 172; © Nadine Greef, pp. ii, viii, 58, 67, 86, 110–111, 132, 156, 179; © Annie Martin pp. 28–29, 51, 72, 169; © Darren Muir, pp. vi, 16, 33, 62, 70–71, 141, 152–153, 190–191, 198, 212; © Andrew Purcell pp. x, 1, 39, 92–93, 98; © Elysa Weitala pp. 8–9; © Marija Vidal, p. 208

Paperback ISBN: 978-1-638-78197-4
eBook ISBN: 978-1-638-78702-0
R0

FOR SCARLETT,
MY LITTLE CHEF-IN-TRAINING

CONTENTS

INTRODUCTION

I have loved cooking for as long as I can remember. When I met my husband, James, we would spend hours in our tiny kitchen preparing tedious, complicated gourmet dishes, such as 48-hour braised pork belly, Mexican mole with a mile-long list of ingredients, and brown butter gnocchi made entirely from scratch.

Now that we're raising an active one-year-old, spending hours in the kitchen is not an option most of the time. Plus, as I have learned in my years of cooking, less is more. Sometimes it's best to focus on the flavors of fewer ingredients and transform them into something extraordinary.

As a working mom, I face the challenges of cooking fresh meals from scratch during the hectic workweek. Coming up with dinner plans each night can be stressful, which is why so many of us give in to the temptations of convenient processed foods, fast food, and takeout. Because let's face it: After a hard day's work, I want to avoid a frantic, last-minute rush to the store and hurried dinner prep. My solution? I rely on a repertoire of simple, tried-and-true staples that my family loves, which makes meal preparation stress-free and grocery shopping a breeze.

Whether you're a seasoned home cook who wants to add easy meal ideas to your recipe repertoire or a beginner who is unsure where to start in the kitchen, I will show everything you need to succeed. With the help of this book, you'll confidently prepare delicious, satisfying meals for yourself or your family.

With a treasure trove of easy, delicious recipes requiring only five ingredients, plus a few freebie pantry staples (salt, pepper, oil, and water), you can whip up breakfast, lunch, dinner, snacks, and even desserts any day of the week. Better still, the ingredients found in these recipes store well in the pantry, refrigerator, or freezer, making them the perfect foundation for easy, last-minute meals.

Throughout the book, I provide tips and suggestions to help you make these recipes your own. My hope is that the time you spend cooking will be more enjoyable because the food coming out of your kitchen is delicious and easier to prepare. With the help of the recipes and ideas in this book, you'll feel inspired and confident when you open the refrigerator and see a random assortment of ingredients, because you'll know how to create your own healthy, delicious recipes with five ingredients or fewer. Happy cooking!

1

THE 5-INGREDIENT KITCHEN

All the recipes in this book use five ingredients or fewer, although a few pantry staples don't count toward this total—salt, pepper, water, and oil. Some recipes include optional ingredients that you can add for more flavor, but they aren't necessary to make the recipe tasty. Five-ingredient recipes allow you to whip up a delicious meal at a moment's notice without making a separate trip to the grocery store. Once you have these building blocks, you'll use them repeatedly to create a variety of mouthwatering meals.

STOCKING UP FOR 5-INGREDIENT COOKING

Having a well-stocked kitchen makes five-ingredient cooking a snap. Don't worry if you don't have all or even most of the ingredients here. Use this list as a guide for the items you could add to your next shopping list; you'll accumulate them as you make the recipes that appeal to you. You can then decide how much of an ingredient you'd need in your kitchen depending on how often you use it.

IN THE PANTRY

Pantry staples are the ingredients you should always have because they are used commonly in cooking. They should be shelf-stable or could be kept in the refrigerator for weeks without spoiling. Most importantly, these ingredients will be used often to ensure you get your money's worth.

BAKING POWDER—Baking powder is a multipurpose leavening agent and a staple in any baker's pantry. Baking powder has a shelf life of six months to a year and is particularly sensitive to moisture, so be sure to store it in a cool and dry place.

CANNED BEANS—Canned beans are convenient, versatile, and have a long shelf life. Keep some canned black beans, chickpeas, and cannellini beans in your pantry for easy, nutritious meals.

DRIED HERBS AND SPICES—Cooking with aromatic ingredients such as chili powder, cinnamon, cumin, dried thyme, and dried oregano elevates the flavor of dishes. Just remember, it's important that your dried herbs and spices are not too old because they tend to lose their potency and flavor after sitting in the pantry for years.

DRIED PASTA—This is a quick and easy go-to pantry staple. Feel free to stock up on a few varieties of long pasta (such as spaghetti and fettuccine) and short pasta (such as penne and macaroni).

FLOUR—All-purpose flour is mostly used in savory and sweet dishes. Self-rising flour, which contains salt and baking powder, is used in several recipes in this book for simple baking.

GARLIC—A little goes a long way with garlic. You can usually find jars of preminced raw garlic, but, if time allows, peeling and mincing fresh garlic is worth the extra effort.

OIL—Extra-virgin olive oil is an absolute essential in the pantry. It is used for sautéing and roasting and as a base for salad dressings, among many other things. Vegetable oil is sometimes used in dishes where a neutral flavor is desired.

ONIONS—Many savory recipes in this book include onions. I typically purchase yellow onions, but white onions work well, too. Red onions are milder and can be eaten raw with salads, for instance.

POTATOES—I always have potatoes on hand and use them in everything from oven fries and breakfast hashes to mashed potatoes and stews. Some are starchier than others, so experiment with different varieties of potatoes for different uses.

SWEET POTATOES—Sweet potatoes last about two weeks when stored properly in a cool, dark, and dry space. I use sweet potatoes in a variety of sweet and savory dishes, whether they are baked and topped with a pat of butter or added to chili to turn it into a filling main dish.

RICE—A foundational ingredient that you can serve in so many ways, rice can be kept at room temperature for a long time if stored properly, making it smart to buy it in bulk.

ROLLED OATS—Also called old-fashioned oats, they have a chewy texture and hold their shape well once cooked. Rolled oats are a good choice for making cookies, cakes, muffins, and granola.

SALT—Salt brings out the flavor in dishes and should be used sparingly; add more to taste if needed. I use kosher salt for almost all the recipes in this book, and I always have some coarse sea salt for finishing a dish.

SOY SAUCE—A key ingredient to many recipes and dishes, soy sauce adds a rich umami flavor. I like to use low-sodium soy sauce to have more control over salt levels.

SWEETENERS—Honey, maple syrup, and brown sugar are used to add sweetness and depth to desserts, beverages, and other dishes.

VINEGAR—Balsamic vinegar packs a flavor punch and helps balance sweet and savory dishes with its acidity. Red and white wine vinegar are mild, and rice vinegar is slightly sweet and delicate.

IN THE REFRIGERATOR

These fresh ingredients serve as the backbone to many of the recipes in this book and are what I use daily to build my meals.

BUTTER—My favorite fat for baking is butter. Unsalted butter is always a better pick when you are cooking so that you can control the amount of salt in your recipe.

CHEESE—Parmesan cheese adds a nutty flavor to dishes like omelets, pastas, and cream-based sauces, whereas sharp Cheddar, with its intense, savory flavor, can be used in breakfasts, salads, casseroles, and as a garnish for soup. For the freshest taste, try to purchase cheese in block form instead of grated or shredded.

EGGS—Eggs are essential in the kitchen whether cooking or baking, and you will find plenty of use for them in breakfast, lunch, and dinner recipes.

FRESH HERBS—The recipes in this book sometimes call for parsley, cilantro, basil, thyme, and rosemary to add a pop of freshness to a dish. If you only have dried herbs, a good rule of thumb when substituting dried for fresh herbs is to use one-third the amount of fresh herb.

GREEK YOGURT—Serve atop morning granola with fresh fruit. Greek yogurt can also be a lighter substitute for sour cream or mayonnaise.

MILK—Milk adds richness and depth to dishes. Unsweetened coconut milk and almond milk are good dairy-free milk substitutes.

PRODUCE—I always have a wide range of fruits and vegetables on standby, including ones that last for a while without spoiling such as apples, sweet potatoes, and carrots, and ones that are best eaten fresh like kale and bell peppers. Prewashed spinach is a convenient and versatile vegetable that can be added to so many dishes and recipes for a nutrient boost. You can also keep a handful of fruits readily available as a delicious snack or to complement your breakfast.

IN THE FREEZER

The recipes in this book do not rely heavily on frozen ingredients. However, frozen ingredients are good to have as backup, because they make cooking at home much easier and save you a last-minute trip to the grocery store.

FROZEN FRUITS—When fresh fruits are not available or in season, frozen fruits can be a good option. Frozen blueberries, strawberries, and peaches can be used in smoothies, breakfast items, and desserts.

FROZEN PROTEIN—Fresh meats can be frozen for months and defrosted before cooking. I like to keep a few protein options in my freezer, such as chicken breasts or thighs, lean ground beef or turkey, and pork sausages.

FROZEN VEGETABLES—Not only are frozen vegetables an excellent budget saver, but they are also convenient and ready to be used in recipes. Adding frozen peas and spinach is an easy way to incorporate vegetables into a dish year-round, even if they aren't in season.

THE POWER PANTRY

Some ingredients really pack a flavor punch and are great to have on hand, whereas others are useful shortcut ingredients that save time. Here are some of my favorites:

BROTH. Often used in soups and sauces, vegetable, chicken, or beef broths are ultrapractical ingredients I love to keep in my pantry for their flavor-enhancing properties.

FRESH LEMON. Fresh lemon juice and zest add brightness and acidity that the bottled variety cannot.

NONSTICK COOKING SPRAY. I like to use canola oil cooking spray for cooking and baking because its neutral flavor makes it ideal for a variety of meals.

PESTO. Keep a jar or two of ready-to-use basil or sun-dried tomato pesto in your pantry to use as a pasta sauce or sandwich spread in a pinch.

ROASTED WHOLE NUTS. Choose lightly salted or unsalted nuts to add texture and crunch to dishes. Store in an airtight container in the refrigerator to maintain freshness.

SRIRACHA. A dash of this tangy, spicy sauce adds an instant yum factor and makes everything taste a little better.

TAHINI. Made from sesame seeds, tahini adds creaminess and nutty flavor to hummus and dips.

VANILLA EXTRACT. Choose a high-quality vanilla extract (choose pure extract, and avoid the imitation kind) because it plays a supporting role in so many recipes and the difference in taste is extraordinary.

WINE. Wine adds complexity to dishes that water or broth can't. Opt for dry wine varietals, such as sauvignon blanc and merlot, in savory dishes to build depth and flavor.

ABOUT THE RECIPES

The recipes in this book are all designed to be easy to prepare with just five ingredients or fewer. Remember: salt, pepper, oil/nonstick cooking spray, water, and optional ingredients do not count toward the five ingredients. The cooking methods are meant to be easy, too. With so few ingredients, prep time is usually 15 minutes or less. You will also find both quick-cooking recipes and recipes that have longer, hands-off cooking time on the stovetop or in the oven.

A wide variety of recipes will cater to different types of dietary preferences. To help with meal planning, keep an eye out for the following labels:

30 MINUTES OR LESS: These recipes can be prepped, cooked, and served in 30 minutes or less.

DAIRY-FREE: Do not contain any cow's milk products or ingredients.

GLUTEN-FREE: Do not have any grains that contain gluten such as wheat, barley, or rye. That said, some ingredients, like canned vegetables, sauces, and seasonings, may contain trace amounts of gluten from processing, so if you have any doubts, be sure to check the ingredient label.

NUT-FREE: Do not contain peanuts, tree nuts, nut butters, or nut-containing ingredients, except for coconut, which is technically a fruit.

ONE POT: All the ingredients are cooked or prepared in a single vessel, such as a pot, pan, or baking dish.

VEGAN: Do not contain any animal by-products, including dairy, eggs, and honey.

VEGETARIAN: Do not contain meat, poultry, game, fish, shellfish, or animal proteins. For the purpose of this book, recipes labeled vegetarian may contain dairy products or eggs.

Finally, at the end of each recipe, you will find helpful tips on prepping, cooking, using alternative ingredients to modify the dish, or substituting ingredients.

Cooking appetizing meals at home should be approachable and fun, and I hope you discover how true that is in every recipe in this book. Ready to get started?

➡️ SHEET PAN
FRENCH TOAST

P. 19

2

BREAKFAST

ORANGE DREAM SMOOTHIE

MAKES: 2 (14-ounce) servings   **PREP TIME:** 5 minutes

Whip up this easy, dairy-free smoothie for a grab-and-go breakfast or afternoon snack. I especially love how the citrusy flavor accents the sweetness of the carrot. With no added sugar and a dose of vegetable from the carrots, this smoothie is bursting with vibrant flavors and nutrients. Your morning is about to get a little better.

2 oranges, peeled	**½ cup chopped carrots**	**½ cup coconut milk**
1 banana, halved and frozen	**¼ cup raw cashews**	**1 cup water**

1. Put the oranges, banana, carrots, cashews, coconut milk, and water in a blender. Blend at high speed until smooth.
2. Divide the smoothie evenly between 2 cups, and serve.

VARIATION TIP: Using a ripe banana will already sweeten this smoothie, but if you want it sweeter still, add a little honey or maple syrup (as a vegan option).

Per Serving: Calories: 340; Total fat: 20g; Saturated fat: 12g; Protein: 7g; Carbs: 40g; Sugar: 21g; Fiber: 6g; Sodium: 30mg

BROWN SUGAR OATMEAL MUG CAKE

SERVES: 1 **PREP TIME:** 5 minutes **COOK TIME:** 2 minutes

This mug cake is the perfect breakfast treat when you're craving a little something sweet. In only a few minutes, you can be indulging in a scrumptious, moist, single-size breakfast cake. If you've never made cake in the microwave, you're in for a delicious treat!

¼ cup rolled oats

2 tablespoons
all-purpose flour

1 tablespoon brown sugar

¼ teaspoon baking powder

3 tablespoons milk

1 tablespoon vegetable oil

1. In a ramekin or standard 8-ounce mug, stir together the oats, flour, sugar, baking powder, milk, and oil until well combined and smooth.

2. Microwave on high for 1 to 1½ minutes, or until cooked through, and serve.

VARIATION TIP: Add a dash of cinnamon to this recipe for a rich, warm flavor.

Per Serving: Calories: 301; Total fat: 17g; Saturated fat: 2g; Protein: 7g; Carbs: 39g; Sugar: 11g; Fiber: 4g; Sodium: 118mg

BLUEBERRY CIDER QUICK BREAD

MAKES: 1 loaf (8 slices)   **PREP TIME**: 10 minutes   **COOK TIME**: 1 hour

If you enjoy beer bread, you need to try this recipe. It uses hard cider to help the bread rise and give it great flavor. I like to use hard apple cider, but feel free to get creative with flavors you like, such as pear, raspberry, and even pumpkin spice cider. If you'd like to make this alcohol-free, see the tip at the end.

Nonstick cooking spray, for coating the loaf pan	2⅔ cups self-rising flour ¼ cup light brown sugar	1 (12-ounce) can hard cider 1 cup blueberries

1. Preheat the oven to 375°F. Grease an 8-by-4-inch loaf pan with cooking spray.

2. To make the batter, in a large mixing bowl, stir together the flour and sugar.

3. Stir in the hard cider until fully combined, followed by the blueberries.

4. Pour the batter into the prepared loaf pan. Tap gently to even it out.

5. Transfer the loaf pan to the oven, and bake for 50 minutes to 1 hour, or until a knife inserted into the loaf comes out clean. Remove from the oven. Let cool.

6. Turn the bread out onto a platter, slice, and serve.

VARIATION TIP: Don't want to use hard cider? Substitute club soda, and add 1 teaspoon each vanilla extract and ground cinnamon to the recipe.

Per Serving (1 slice): Calories: 204; Total fat: 0g; Saturated fat: 0g; Protein: 4g; Carbs: 42g; Sugar: 9g; Fiber: 2g; Sodium: 502mg

PEACH MUESLI

(NF) (OP) (V)

SERVES: 4   **PREP TIME:** 10 minutes, plus overnight to chill

For a change of pace from overnight oats, try this overnight muesli. It's the perfect make-ahead breakfast! I like to assemble the night before in a Mason jar for a delicious grab-and-go treat. You can also prepare it first thing in the morning if you have an hour or more to let it rest.

2 cups plain Greek yogurt	**2 tablespoons maple**	**2 ripe peaches, pitted and**
2 cups rolled oats	**syrup**	**coarsely chopped**
½ cup unsweetened		
shredded coconut		

1. In a large resealable container, stir together the yogurt, oats, coconut, and maple syrup. Seal the container, and refrigerate overnight.

2. Stir in the peaches in the morning, and serve.

COOKING TIP: For a deeper, richer flavor, try toasting the shredded coconut before stirring it into this simple breakfast. Preheat the oven to 250°F. Spread the shredded coconut out on a sheet pan. Toast in the oven, stirring occasionally, for about 15 minutes total, or until the coconut is golden brown and fragrant. Store the toasted coconut in a sealed container for up to 2 weeks.

VARIATION TIP: Try your own variations of muesli from a combination of any yogurt, dried and fresh fruit, oats, nuts, seeds, and sweeteners (even chocolate chips).

Per Serving: Calories: 378; Total fat: 11g; Saturated fat: 6g; Protein: 14g; Carbs: 57g; Sugar: 19g; Fiber: 8g; Sodium: 61mg

BAKED OATMEAL WITH STRAWBERRIES AND ALMOND BUTTER

SERVES: 4 **PREP TIME:** 10 minutes **COOK TIME:** 30 minutes

Traditional stovetop oatmeal has a creamy porridge consistency, whereas baked oatmeal combines chewy, soft, and creamy textures all in one casserole dish. You can change your mix-ins each time while following the same formula. Just throw in what you have stocked in the refrigerator and pantry or what's in season. Blueberries and cashew butter are another awesome combination to try.

---

2 cups unsweetened almond or cashew milk

¼ cup almond butter

2 cups rolled oats

1 cup coarsely chopped fresh strawberries

1 teaspoon baking powder

---

1. Preheat the oven to 350°F. Line an 8-by-8-inch baking pan with parchment paper.

2. To make the batter, in a large bowl, blend the almond milk and almond butter by hand until smooth.

3. Stir in the oats, strawberries, and baking powder.

4. Spoon the batter into the prepared pan.

5. Transfer the pan to the oven, and bake for about 30 minutes, or until the oatmeal is firm and golden. Remove from the oven. Let cool for 10 minutes, and serve.

VARIATION TIP: Jazz up this recipe with chopped nuts, dried cranberries, quinoa, or wheat berries, and serve it with a drizzle of maple syrup and a huge dollop of whipped coconut cream.

Per Serving: Calories: 342; Total fat: 14g; Saturated fat: 1g; Protein: 15g; Carbs: 44g; Sugar: 3g; Fiber: 9g; Sodium: 115mg

HOMEMADE GRANOLA

MAKES: 15 ounces   **PREP TIME:** 5 minutes   **COOK TIME:** 15 minutes

Everyone needs a trusty homemade granola recipe in their repertoire. Granola is great to prepare on a Sunday to enjoy during the week. It's fantastic as part of a yogurt parfait or with a splash of milk. You can also preportion the granola in single-serving-size snack containers to take on the go.

1 cup rolled oats

1 cup walnuts, chopped

½ cup shredded coconut

¼ cup maple syrup

¼ cup coconut oil

1. Preheat the oven to 400°F. Line a sheet pan with parchment paper.

2. In a bowl, mix together the oats, walnuts, and shredded coconut thoroughly.

3. In a small saucepan, combine the maple syrup and coconut oil. Bring just to a boil. Remove from the heat. Pour over the dry mixture, and mix to combine.

4. Spread the granola out in a single layer on the prepared sheet pan.

5. Transfer the sheet pan to the oven, and bake for 15 minutes. Remove from the oven. Let the granola cool completely before storing in a glass container with a lid.

SUBSTITUTION TIP: You can use any type of nut for this granola. Almonds and hazelnuts work great. You can also use sunflower seeds if you wish to make the granola nut-free. Honey can be used instead of maple syrup, too.

Per Serving (3 ounces): Calories: 389; Total fat: 30g; Saturated fat: 13g; Protein: 7g; Carbs: 27g; Sugar: 11g; Fiber: 4g; Sodium: 4mg

YOGURT-CHIA PUDDING

(30) (GF) (NF) (OP) (V)

SERVES: 1 **PREP TIME:** 5 minutes, plus 20 minutes to rest

Perfectly thick, creamy, and rich, this yogurt pudding tastes almost like a dessert! It's so easy to throw together, too. Storing it in your refrigerator in single-serving portions makes it so convenient to grab when you need a quick breakfast or snack.

¾ cup plain Greek yogurt	1 tablespoon maple syrup	Fruit of choice, for topping
3 tablespoons chia seeds	½ teaspoon vanilla extract	(optional)

1. In a glass bowl or jar with a lid, combine the yogurt, chia seeds, maple syrup, and vanilla. Stir until well combined. Cover, and let rest for about 20 minutes on the kitchen counter or in the refrigerator.

2. Mix and add your favorite fruit toppings (if using).

✳ VARIATION TIP: Use flavored Greek yogurt, add fresh or dried fruit for a flavor boost, or both. Try a tropical version with coconut yogurt topped with chopped fresh mango.

Per Serving: Calories: 377; Total fat: 19g; Saturated fat: 5g; Protein: 13g; Carbs: 40g; Sugar: 21g; Fiber: 15g; Sodium: 94mg

SHEET PAN FRENCH TOAST

SERVES: 4   **PREP TIME:** 10 minutes   **COOK TIME:** 15 to 20 minutes

Instead of having to cook each French toast one by one on the stove, this baked French toast is made in a sheet pan, and everything gets cooked at the same time. It's a recipe you can double when serving a crowd. It doesn't get easier than that!

Nonstick cooking spray, for coating the sheet pan

2 large eggs

½ cup milk

1 teaspoon vanilla extract

½ teaspoon ground cinnamon

8 brioche or challah bread slices

---

1. Preheat the oven to 375°F. Spray a large sheet pan with cooking spray.

2. In a shallow bowl, whisk together the eggs, milk, vanilla, and cinnamon.

3. Dip a slice of bread into the egg mixture, turning to coat both sides. Let the excess egg mixture drip back into the bowl. Place the egg-dipped bread on the prepared sheet pan. Repeat with the remaining bread slices.

4. Transfer the sheet pan to the oven, and bake for 10 minutes.

5. Remove the sheet pan from the oven, and flip each slice of bread. If needed, spray the sheet pan with more cooking spray.

6. Return the sheet pan to the oven, and bake for 5 to 6 minutes, or until the bread is crispy and golden brown. Remove from the oven.

7. Serve the French toast hot with any optional toppings (see tip), and enjoy.

VARIATION TIP: Add some extra flavor by topping the French toast with fresh fruit, such as sliced bananas, strawberries, or blueberries, and a dusting of powdered sugar.

Per Serving: Calories: 208; Total fat: 5g; Saturated fat: 2g; Protein: 9g; Carbs: 30g; Sugar: 5g; Fiber: 2g; Sodium: 323mg

TOFU-PEPPER SCRAMBLE

(30) (DF) (GF) (NF) (OP) (VG)

SERVES: 2   **PREP TIME:** 5 minutes   **COOK TIME:** 10 minutes

Tofu is something we eat regularly at our house, especially when we want to have a protein-packed, plant-based meal. This dish makes for a flavorful, satisfying breakfast—one that's guaranteed to keep you full until lunch. I love topping this with a spoonful of salsa and sliced avocado. Even if you're not vegan, I hope you'll give it a try.

---

1 tablespoon vegetable oil	**¼ cup diced red bell pepper**	**1 (14-ounce) package**
¼ cup diced onion	**Kosher salt**	**firm tofu**
¼ cup diced green bell pepper	**Freshly ground black pepper**	

---

1. Warm a medium nonstick skillet over medium heat.

2. Pour in the oil, and add the onion, green bell pepper, and red bell pepper. Season with salt and black pepper. Cook for about 5 minutes, or until the peppers soften and the onion starts to turn translucent.

3. Add the tofu, and break it up using a spoon. Cook for 3 to 4 minutes, or until the tofu is hot. Remove from the heat. Serve.

✳ **PREP TIP:** Be sure to choose firm or extra-firm tofu so that the crumbles hold their shape as you cook. Do not substitute with medium or silken tofu because it is too soft and will fall apart as you cook it. You don't need to drain the tofu because firm tofu has less water in it and doesn't affect the dish.

Per Serving: Calories: 397; Total fat: 26g; Saturated fat: 4g; Protein: 35g; Carbs: 13g; Sugar: 2g; Fiber: 6g; Sodium: 110mg

WESTERN EGG BREAKFAST MUFFINS

SERVES: 4 **PREP TIME:** 5 minutes **COOK TIME:** 20 minutes

These egg muffins are a simple and delicious way to add some variety into your breakfast routine. My family loves them so I always make a big batch and freeze some to enjoy later whenever we need a quick breakfast or snack. They're perfect on their own if you're looking for a low-carb breakfast, or tuck them inside an English muffin or between slices of toast for something more substantial.

Nonstick cooking spray, for coating the muffin tin

8 large eggs

1 teaspoon water

6 ounces diced ham

1 red bell pepper, cored and chopped

½ cup shredded Cheddar cheese

Kosher salt

Freshly ground black pepper

1. Preheat the oven to 350°F. Spray 8 cups of a 12-cup muffin tin with cooking spray.

2. In a large bowl, whisk together the eggs, water, ham, bell pepper, and cheese. Season with salt and pepper.

3. Pour the egg mixture into the prepared muffin cups.

4. Transfer the muffin tin to the oven, and bake for 20 minutes. Remove from the oven. Place on a wire rack. Let cool before removing the muffins from the tins. Serve warm.

VARIATION TIP: You can use any of your favorite vegetables to personalize these muffins. A few of my favorites include broccoli, mushrooms, and baby spinach.

Per Serving: Calories: 279; Total fat: 18g; Saturated fat: 7g; Protein: 23g; Carbs: 4g; Sugar: 2g; Fiber: 1g; Sodium: 759mg

EGG-IN-A-HASH WITH SWEET POTATO AND BACON

SERVES: 4 **PREP TIME:** 10 minutes **COOK TIME:** 20 to 25 minutes

Every sweet and savory bite of this breakfast hash is unforgettably delicious. The fact that it cooks in one skillet is a bonus, which you'll appreciate when it's time to clean up. Although a cast-iron pan produces the nicest browning on the bottom of the hash, you can still use other types of skillets for this recipe.

---

4 bacon slices

2 large sweet potatoes, peeled and diced

½ cup diced onion

2 teaspoons fresh rosemary leaves, minced

1 teaspoon kosher salt, plus more for seasoning

½ teaspoon freshly ground black pepper, plus more for seasoning

4 large eggs

---

1. Preheat the oven to 400°F.

2. Put the bacon in a large cast-iron pan (or another oven-safe pan), and cook over medium-low heat for 6 to 7 minutes, or until crisp. Transfer to paper towels to drain. Reserving 2 tablespoons, pour off the bacon fat from the pan.

3. Increase the heat to medium. Add the sweet potatoes and onion to the pan. Cover, and cook, stirring occasionally, for 5 to 6 minutes.

4. Turn off the heat. Crumble the bacon into the pan, and add the rosemary, salt, and pepper. Stir to combine.

5. Make 4 wells in the mixture, and crack an egg into each one. Sprinkle the eggs with a little salt and pepper if desired.

6. Transfer the pan to the oven, and bake for 6 to 10 minutes, depending on whether you prefer the yolks runny or cooked through. Remove from the oven. Serve immediately.

SUBSTITUTION TIP: To make it vegetarian, leave out the bacon; cook the onion and sweet potatoes in 2 tablespoons olive oil.

COOKING TIP: When sweet potatoes are cooked in cast iron, the natural sugars tend to burn quickly. Watch carefully, and adjust the heat to avoid burning.

Per Serving: Calories: 190; Total fat: 9g; Saturated fat: 3g; Protein: 11g; Carbs: 15g; Sugar: 4g; Fiber: 2g; Sodium: 883mg

SHAKSHUKA

(30) (DF) (GF) (NF) (OP) (V)

SERVES: 4   **PREP TIME:** 10 minutes   **COOK TIME:** 15 minutes

Shakshuka is essentially poached eggs in a seasoned tomato sauce. This quick-and-easy version is a little different from the traditional Mediterranean dish because it includes kale instead of peppers. Serve it as is, or garnish with some fresh parsley and pair it with pita or crusty bread.

---

2 tablespoons extra-virgin
  olive oil
1 onion, halved and
  thinly sliced

4 cups chopped
  stemmed kale
¼ teaspoon ground oregano
Kosher salt

Freshly ground black pepper
1 (15-ounce) can fire-roasted
  diced tomatoes, drained
4 large eggs

---

1. In a skillet, heat the oil over medium heat.

2. Add the onion, and cook for 5 minutes, or until soft.

3. Stir in the kale and oregano. Season with salt and pepper. Cook, stirring often, for about 2 minutes, or until the kale is wilted and tender.

4. Add the tomatoes, and bring to a simmer.

5. Make 4 indentations in the mixture, and crack an egg into each one. Cook for about 5 minutes, or until the whites have set but the yolks are still runny. Remove from the heat. Serve.

PREP TIP: Put your onion in the freezer for 30 minutes before cutting it to prevent those onion tears.

VARIATION TIP: This tomato-based dish is delicious with crumbled feta cheese on top.

Per Serving: Calories: 167; Total fat: 12g; Saturated fat: 3g; Protein: 8g; Carbs: 8g; Sugar: 4g; Fiber: 3g; Sodium: 239mg

CANADIAN BACON AND MUSHROOM FRITTATA

SERVES: 4   **PREP TIME:** 10 minutes   **COOK TIME:** 20 minutes

The beauty of the frittata, besides the ease of preparation, is that it is adaptable to almost any palate. If Canadian bacon and mushrooms aren't your thing, branch out to other mix-ins, such as breakfast sausage, zucchini, or asparagus. I like to eat a wedge on top of a piece of toast for an easy lunch. If you like the idea of breakfast for dinner, try serving a frittata with a bright green salad to round out the meal.

1 tablespoon extra-virgin olive oil	1 red bell pepper, cored and diced	3 cups baby spinach
4 Canadian bacon slices, finely diced	8 ounces cremini mushrooms, thinly sliced	4 large eggs Kosher salt Freshly ground black pepper

1. In a skillet, heat the oil over medium heat until shimmering.
2. Add the bacon and bell pepper. Cook for 7 minutes.
3. Add the mushrooms and spinach. Cook for 3 minutes.
4. In a medium bowl, whisk the eggs. Season with salt and pepper. Pour into the skillet.
5. Reduce the heat to low. Cover, and cook for 7 minutes, or until the top has set. Remove from the heat. Serve.

PREP TIP: Mushrooms absorb water, so to clean them, lightly moisten a paper towel with cool water, and wipe them before cooking.

Per Serving: Calories: 160; Total fat: 9g; Saturated fat: 2g; Protein: 14g; Carbs: 6g; Sugar: 3g; Fiber: 2g; Sodium: 344mg

SAUSAGE, POTATO, AND PEPPER JACK BREAKFAST BAKE

(NF)

SERVES: 6   **PREP TIME:** 10 minutes   **COOK TIME:** 1 hour 10 minutes

When I think of breakfast recipes that feed multiple people, a baked egg casserole comes to mind. Many variations of breakfast bakes have come out of my kitchen over the years, but this one—using frozen diced potatoes as a shortcut—may be the most straightforward, delicious one of all.

---

12 ounces breakfast
    sausage or sausage links,
    casings removed
3 cups frozen diced potatoes

8 large eggs
¾ cup milk
1½ cups shredded pepper
    Jack cheese

Kosher salt
Freshly ground black pepper

---

1. Preheat the oven to 350°F.
2. Put the sausage in a Dutch oven, and cook over medium-high heat, stirring occasionally, for 12 to 16 minutes, or until crispy and brown. Drain in a colander to remove most of the fat, then return to the Dutch oven.
3. Add the potatoes, and cook, stirring occasionally, for 5 minutes.
4. In a large bowl, beat the eggs, and whisk in the milk. Pour over the sausage and potatoes.
5. Sprinkle with the cheese. Remove from the heat.
6. Transfer the pot to the oven, and bake for 40 to 50 minutes, or until the eggs have set and the top of the casserole is brown. Remove from the oven. Season with salt and pepper. Let cool slightly before serving.

VARIATION TIP: If you don't like spicy foods, you can use regular Monterey Jack or Cheddar cheese in this recipe. If, on the other hand, you want it even spicier, add a dash or two of your favorite hot sauce on top.

Per Serving: Calories: 427; Total fat: 27g; Saturated fat: 10g; Protein: 27g; Carbs: 19g; Sugar: 3g; Fiber: 1g; Sodium: 689mg

EASY RUSTIC CORNED BEEF HASH

SERVES: 6   **PREP TIME:** 15 minutes   **COOK TIME:** 40 minutes

Having grown up in New York City, I've had my fair share of corned beef hash from the many famous delis. This classic breakfast, made with savory corned beef, diced potatoes, and peppers, can be made at home and tastes just as good! To make crispy corned beef hash, resist the urge to stir the hash when it's in the pan, and flip it over only when one side has already crisped up.

---

3 cups diced peeled Yukon Gold potatoes

2 tablespoons extra-virgin olive oil

1 small green bell pepper, cored and chopped

2 cups diced corned beef, either leftover or from the deli

2 scallions, both white and green parts, chopped

Kosher salt

Freshly ground black pepper

---

1. Put the potatoes in a Dutch oven, and cover with cold water. Bring to a boil over high heat.

2. Reduce the heat to a simmer. Cook for about 5 minutes, or until the potatoes have slightly softened. Drain in a colander.

3. In the Dutch oven, heat the oil over medium-high heat until shimmering.

4. Add the bell pepper, and cook for 5 minutes, or until softened.

5. Add the potatoes, and spread out in an even layer. Cook for about 10 minutes, or until the bottoms start to brown.

6. Flip the potatoes, and add the corned beef and scallions. Using a wooden spoon, stir to combine. Cook for 10 minutes, allowing the potatoes to evenly brown on the other side. Remove from the heat. Season with salt and pepper before serving.

COOKING TIP: Instead of parboiling the potatoes, you can pierce them with a fork, put them in a microwave-safe bowl covered with a wet paper towel, and microwave on high for 3 to 4 minutes, or until slightly softened.

VARIATION TIP: This hash is delicious with a fried egg on top.

Per Serving: Calories: 196; Total fat: 12g; Saturated fat: 3g; Protein: 9g; Carbs: 14g; Sugar: 1g; Fiber: 2g; Sodium: 399mg

➥

LEMONY OLIVES AND
FETA MEDLEY

P. 41

3

APPETIZERS AND SNACKS

SMOKY EGGPLANT DIP

MAKES: 1¼ cups   **PREP TIME:** 10 minutes   **COOK TIME:** 30 minutes

This eggplant dip is a version of baba ghanoush, a Middle Eastern and Mediterranean eggplant dip that's traditionally served with pita bread and crisp vegetables. Making baba ghanoush is a very similar process to making hummus—you're basically swapping out the chickpeas called for in hummus for roasted eggplant. Smooth, smoky, and savory, it can be served chilled or at room temperature. Try using it as a sandwich spread to jazz up your lunch.

---

1 large globe eggplant

2 tablespoons tahini

1 lemon, juiced

2 garlic cloves, peeled

2 tablespoons extra-virgin olive oil

½ teaspoon ground cumin

Kosher salt

Freshly ground black pepper

1 or 2 tablespoons water

---

1. Preheat the oven to 350°F.

2. Using a fork, poke holes in the eggplant 2 or 3 times, and put the eggplant on a sheet pan.

3. Transfer the sheet pan to the oven, and bake for 25 to 30 minutes, or until the eggplant has softened. Remove from the oven. Let cool.

4. Once cool enough to handle, peel the skin off the eggplant, and put the flesh in a blender.

5. Add the tahini, lemon juice, garlic, oil, and cumin. Season with salt and pepper. Process until smooth, adding the water as needed.

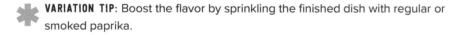 **VARIATION TIP:** Boost the flavor by sprinkling the finished dish with regular or smoked paprika.

Per Serving (¼ cup): Calories: 116; Total fat: 9g; Saturated fat: 1g; Protein: 2g; Carbs: 9g; Sugar: 4g; Fiber: 4g; Sodium: 10mg

BUTTERNUT SQUASH HUMMUS

MAKES: 2 cups   **PREP TIME:** 10 minutes   **COOK TIME:** 20 to 25 minutes

Making perfect hummus at home can be a hit or miss. I've made too many batches of dense, grainy hummus to know that the extra step of boiling canned chickpeas makes all the difference! You'll be rewarded with a smooth, creamy, and light hummus every time.

---

2 cups diced butternut squash
4 tablespoons extra-virgin olive oil, divided
Kosher salt

Freshly ground black pepper
1 (15-ounce) can chickpeas, drained
2 tablespoons tahini
½ cup plain Greek yogurt

2 tablespoons cold water
1 teaspoon ground cinnamon, plus more for garnish

---

1. Preheat the oven to 400°F.

2. Arrange the butternut squash on a large sheet pan. Drizzle with 1 tablespoon of oil. Season with salt and pepper.

3. Transfer the sheet pan to the oven, and roast, turning once halfway through, for 15 to 20 minutes, or until the squash is golden brown and fork tender. Remove from the oven. Let cool.

4. Meanwhile, put the chickpeas in a small saucepan, and cover with water. Bring to a boil over medium heat. Reduce the heat to low. Cook for about 20 minutes, or until the chickpeas are soft. Remove from the heat. Drain in a colander.

5. Put the chickpeas, squash, tahini, yogurt, water, 2 tablespoons of oil, and cinnamon in a food processor. Blend until smooth. If too thick, add more olive oil or water. Season with salt.

6. Serve the hummus in a shallow bowl, drizzled with the remaining 1 tablespoon of oil and garnished with a sprinkle of cinnamon.

✳ **SUBSTITUTION TIP:** Pumpkin would be delicious in this recipe. Substitute pumpkin for butternut squash or use ¾ cup pumpkin puree as a shortcut, and blend with the rest of the ingredients in step 6.

Per Serving (¼ cup): Calories: 158; Total fat: 10g; Saturated fat: 2g; Protein: 4g; Carbs: 14g; Sugar: 3g; Fiber: 4g; Sodium: 34mg

CHEDDAR CHEESE AND BEER DIP

(30) (NF) (OP) (V)

MAKES: about 6 cups   **PREP TIME:** 10 minutes   **COOK TIME:** 20 minutes

This is the ultimate game-day appetizer. And the best part? The beer you choose will completely alter the flavor of this dip. Replace the lager with pilsner or ale for a mild, subtle flavor. Choose an IPA if you're feeling like something hoppy or dark beers like stout and malt if you want something richer. Nonalcoholic beers work just fine in this recipe, too!

1½ cups Mexican-style lager beer

1 (14-ounce) can diced tomatoes with green chiles

1 (8-ounce) package cream cheese

4 cups shredded Cheddar cheese blend

1 (16-ounce) bag corn tortilla chips

---

1. In a Dutch oven, bring the beer to a boil over medium-high heat.

2. Reduce the heat to medium-low. Add the tomatoes with green chiles and the cream cheese. Stir constantly until the cream cheese has melted.

3. Add the shredded cheese by the handful, stirring constantly after each addition, until all the cheese has melted into the sauce. Cook for 10 to 15 minutes, or until the dip is bubbly. Remove from the heat. Transfer to a serving dish.

4. Serve the dip with the tortilla chips.

✳ **COOKING TIP:** I keep the dip right on the stove and fill a serving dish as necessary. You can turn the heat on low when the dip needs to be warmed up a bit.

Per Serving (½ cup): Calories: 414; Total fat: 27g; Saturated fat: 12g; Protein: 13g; Carbs: 29g; Sugar: 1g; Fiber: 2g; Sodium: 569mg

NECTARINE-TOMATO
BRUSCHETTA

P. 34

NECTARINE-TOMATO BRUSCHETTA

(30) (DF) (NF) (VG)

SERVES: 4 **PREP TIME:** 15 minutes **COOK TIME:** 1 minute

Sweet nectarines, juicy tomato, and fresh basil come together for a bright and refreshing bruschetta topping. Pile the mixture on top of toasted baguette pieces, and you have a surefire winner of an appetizer. This is also a wonderful topping for grilled fish or shrimp.

---

2 nectarines, pitted and coarsely chopped

1 large tomato, seeded and finely chopped

½ yellow bell pepper, cored and finely chopped

1 tablespoon finely chopped fresh basil leaves

Sea salt

Freshly ground black pepper

8 French baguette slices

1 tablespoon extra-virgin olive oil

---

1. Set the oven to broil.
2. To make the bruschetta topping, in a medium bowl, stir together the nectarines, tomato, bell pepper, and basil. Season with salt and black pepper.
3. Place the bread slices on a sheet pan, and brush lightly with the oil.
4. Transfer the sheet pan to the oven, and broil for about 1 minute, or until the bread is crispy and lightly golden. Remove from the oven.
5. Using a slotted spoon, evenly divide the bruschetta topping onto the bread, and serve immediately.

✱ **VARIATION TIP:** If you enjoy a little heat in your food, adding hot peppers to this recipe produces excellent results. Add 1 teaspoon chopped hot pepper to the other ingredients in step 2. Jalapeño will provide a milder sensation, whereas a habanero or serrano will have a much stronger kick.

Per Serving: Calories: 230; Total fat: 5g; Saturated fat: 1g; Protein: 8g; Carbs: 40g; Sugar: 9g; Fiber: 3g; Sodium: 383mg

SMOKED SALMON LIME PÂTÉ

SERVES: 6 **PREP TIME:** 15 minutes

If you're ever in need of an elegant dish to make for a cocktail party, look no further. This pâté is a no-brainer as an appetizer, and you can serve it with cucumber slices, celery sticks, or crackers. Because smoked salmon is naturally salty, there is no need to add extra salt.

1 cup low-fat cream cheese

½ cup ricotta cheese

Grated zest and juice of 1 lime

1 tablespoon chopped fresh dill

6 ounces smoked salmon

1. Put the cream cheese and ricotta in a food processor. Pulse until smooth.

2. Add the lime zest, lime juice, and dill. Pulse until blended.

3. Add the salmon, and pulse until combined but still chunky. Transfer the pâté to a container, and store in the refrigerator for up to 1 week.

SUBSTITUTION TIP: Any smoked fish is acceptable for this citrus-infused pâté. Smoked trout has a more delicate flavor than smoked salmon and is available in many stores. If using smoked trout, increase the amount to 8 ounces so that the other ingredients don't overwhelm the fish.

Per Serving: Calories: 155; Total fat: 10g; Saturated fat: 6g; Protein: 11g; Carbs: 5g; Sugar: 3g; Fiber: 0g; Sodium: 728mg

MINI CRAB CAKE BITES

SERVES: 4 **PREP TIME:** 5 minutes **COOK TIME:** 15 minutes

My favorite type of food to make when entertaining is the kind you can pop into your mouth with one hand while holding a cocktail in another. That's where these delicious mini crab cake bites come in. They're a breeze to serve and always seem to disappear quickly. Serve them with lemon wedges and tartar sauce if desired.

1 (6-ounce) can crabmeat, drained and picked over

1 shallot, finely chopped

⅓ cup bread crumbs

½ teaspoon garlic powder

Kosher salt

Freshly ground black pepper

2 tablespoons mayonnaise

2 tablespoons extra-virgin olive oil

1. Preheat the oven to 375°F.

2. In a large mixing bowl, stir together the crabmeat, shallot, bread crumbs, and garlic powder. Season lightly with salt and pepper.

3. Stir in the mayonnaise. Using your hands, form 10 (1-inch) balls.

4. In a large, oven-safe skillet, heat the oil over medium heat.

5. Add the crab cake balls, and brown on all sides. This should take 3 to 4 minutes total. Remove from the heat.

6. Transfer the skillet to the oven, and bake for 10 minutes. Remove from the oven. Let cool for a few minutes before transferring the crab cake bites to a serving dish.

COOKING TIP: Go easy on the salt in this recipe; just a pinch or two should be enough.

VARIATION TIP: You can substitute fresh crabmeat for canned. Either way, you'll have to pick through the crab to remove any bits of shells.

Per Serving: Calories: 175; Total fat: 13g; Saturated fat: 2g; Protein: 9g; Carbs: 6g; Sugar: 1g; Fiber: 0g; Sodium: 267mg

FIRE-ROASTED RED PEPPER DIP

(GF) (NF) (V)

MAKES: 2 cups **PREP TIME:** 20 minutes, plus time to cool **COOK TIME:** 15 minutes

Despite the name of the recipe, there's nothing intimidating about this dip. There are two primary (but simple) steps: roasting the peppers and pureeing the dip. If you prefer a bit of heat, keep some of the seeds in the roasted jalapeño.

---

2 red bell peppers

1 jalapeño

1 cup crumbled feta cheese

1 tablespoon chopped fresh mint leaves

1 to 2 tablespoons extra-virgin olive oil

Kosher salt

Freshly ground black pepper

---

1. Preheat the grill on high heat.

2. Put the bell peppers and jalapeño on the grill. Roast, turning every 2 to 3 minutes, for about 15 minutes, or until the skin is completely black. Remove from the heat. Transfer to a metal bowl, and cover very tightly with plastic wrap. Let sit for 10 minutes.

3. Using a kitchen towel, rub the bell peppers and jalapeño to remove the skin. Remove and discard the stems and seeds. Let cool to room temperature.

4. Put the bell peppers, jalapeño, cheese, mint, and 1 tablespoon of oil in a food processor. Pulse until completely combined. Add the remaining 1 tablespoon of oil if the mixture isn't coming together. Season with salt and black pepper.

COOKING TIP: To make this recipe without a grill, roast the peppers in the oven at 400°F for about 35 minutes.

SUBSTITUTION TIP: Instead of roasting your own peppers, you can buy them jarred at the grocery store. This will save you prep time and cleanup. Just make sure to drain the store-bought peppers well and blot them dry using a paper towel. The liquid they come packed in will thin out the dip.

Per Serving (½ cup): Calories: 148; Total fat: 12g; Saturated fat: 6g; Protein: 6g; Carbs: 5g; Sugar: 4g; Fiber: 1g; Sodium: 385mg

BAKED BRIE WITH CARAMELIZED WALNUTS

SERVES: 6   **PREP TIME:** 5 minutes   **COOK TIME:** 25 minutes

Warm, gooey, melted Brie cheese paired with sweet toppings is a classic combination. This crave-worthy appetizer is a little sweet, a little savory, crunchy, creamy, and so easy to make. Top it with dried cranberries or pomegranate seeds for a festive, holiday version, and watch it disappear off your appetizer table in minutes!

---

1 (8-ounce) Brie wheel

2 tablespoons unsalted butter

¼ cup packed brown sugar

3 tablespoons heavy cream

¾ cup whole walnuts

---

1. Preheat the oven to 350°F.

2. Put the Brie in a small oven-safe skillet or baking dish.

3. In a medium nonstick skillet, melt the butter and sugar over low heat for 5 to 10 minutes, or until bubbly.

4. Stir in the cream and then the walnuts, making sure that the walnuts are fully coated. Remove from the heat. Pour over the Brie.

5. Transfer the skillet with the Brie to the oven. Bake for 10 to 15 minutes, or until the Brie has melted. Remove from the oven.

VARIATION TIP: Add ½ teaspoon ground cinnamon or nutmeg to the sugar and butter in step 3, or try replacing the Brie with Camembert cheese for a more earthy, nutty flavor.

Per Serving: Calories: 303; Total fat: 25g; Saturated fat: 11g; Protein: 10g; Carbs: 11g; Sugar: 10g; Fiber: 1g; Sodium: 244mg

➥

TORTELLINI AND
CAPRESE SALAD
SKEWERS

P. 40

TORTELLINI AND CAPRESE SALAD SKEWERS

MAKES: 6 (12-inch) or 12 (6-inch) skewers   **PREP TIME:** 10 minutes   **COOK TIME:** 10 minutes, plus 10 minutes to cool

These colorful skewers inspired by the classic Caprese salad are fantastic for entertaining. Use small or mini skewers if you are entertaining a larger group or long skewers if you are having fewer guests. To make it ahead, assemble the skewers, and drizzle the vinaigrette over them right before serving.

1 (9-ounce) package refrigerated cheese tortellini

¼ cup extra-virgin olive oil

3 tablespoons balsamic vinegar

Pinch kosher salt

Pinch freshly ground black pepper

1 (8-ounce) package fresh mozzarella balls

1 (10-ounce) container grape tomatoes

1 bunch fresh basil, leaves picked

1. Cook the tortellini according to the package directions. This should take 8 to 10 minutes. Remove from the heat. Drain in a colander, and let cool for 10 minutes.

2. Meanwhile, in a large bowl, whisk together the oil, vinegar, salt, and pepper.

3. Add the mozzarella balls and tomatoes. Toss to combine.

4. Once the tortellini have cooled, gently toss into the mixture.

5. Assemble the skewers by alternating layers of mozzarella, tomatoes, basil, and tortellini until all the ingredients have been used.

✳ VARIATION TIP: For a spicy version, add a pinch of red pepper flakes to the oil-and-vinegar mixture.

Per Serving: Calories: 340; Total fat: 21g; Saturated fat: 8g; Protein: 15g; Carbs: 24g; Sugar: 3g; Fiber: 1g; Sodium: 440mg

LEMONY OLIVES AND FETA MEDLEY

(30) (GF) (NF) (V)

SERVES: 8 **PREP TIME:** 10 minutes

When you only have a few minutes to throw together a tasty appetizer or snack, this quick marinated olives and feta recipe will do the trick. I love the salty, briny flavor of olives and always have a jar or two in my pantry. Almost any type of olive will work, so you can choose your favorite type for this recipe.

---

1 (1-pound) block Greek feta cheese, cut into ½-inch dice

3 cups mixed pitted olives (Kalamata, black, or green), drained from brine

¼ cup extra-virgin olive oil

3 tablespoons freshly squeezed lemon juice

1 teaspoon grated lemon zest

1 teaspoon dried oregano

Pita bread, for serving

---

1. In a large bowl, combine the cheese and olives.
2. To make the dressing, in a small bowl, whisk together the oil, lemon juice, lemon zest, and oregano.
3. Pour the dressing over the cheese and olives, and gently toss together to evenly coat.
4. Serve the medley with pita bread.

VARIATION TIP: For a kick of heat, add ½ teaspoon red pepper flakes to the dressing. And instead of serving in a bowl, you can serve the olives and cheese on skewers, adding cherry tomatoes between the olives and cheese.

Per Serving: Calories: 269; Total fat: 24g; Saturated fat: 10g; Protein: 9g; Carbs: 6g; Sugar: 2g; Fiber: 2g; Sodium: 891mg

VEGETABLE CHIPS WITH ROSEMARY SALT (DF) (GF) (NF) (VG)

SERVES: 4   **PREP TIME:** 15 minutes, plus 10 minutes to sweat   **COOK TIME:** 50 minutes

Salty and crunchy, vegetable chips are an incredibly satisfying snack. And the best part is that you can make chips with different vegetables. Here, I used beets, zucchini, sweet potato, and rutabaga, but carrots and parsnips work well, too. Don't skip using salt to sweat the vegetables; removing as much moisture as possible from the vegetables is essential to getting that satisfying crunch.

Olive oil cooking spray, for coating the sheet pan
2 medium beets, peeled and sliced

1 medium zucchini, sliced
1 medium sweet potato, sliced
1 small rutabaga, peeled and sliced

½ teaspoon kosher salt, plus more to sweat the vegetables
¼ teaspoon dried rosemary

1. Preheat the oven to 300°F. Spray a sheet pan with cooking spray. Line a plate with paper towels.

2. Lay the beets, zucchini, sweet potato, and rutabaga in a single layer on a paper towel. Lightly salt, and let sit for 10 minutes. Blot away any moisture on top with another paper towel.

3. Arrange the vegetables on the prepared sheet pan, and spray with cooking spray.

4. Transfer the sheet pan to the oven, and cook for 30 to 40 minutes, or until the vegetables have browned.

5. Flip the vegetables, and cook for 10 minutes, or until crisp. Remove from the oven. Transfer to the prepared plate to remove any excess oil.

6. In a small bowl, mix together the salt and rosemary.

7. Lightly season the chips with the rosemary salt.

COOKING TIP: Because of differences in size, you may need to cook the chips a little more or a little less; keep a close eye on them toward the end of the cooking time to ensure a browned, crisp chip.

Per Serving: Calories: 74; Total fat: 1g; Saturated fat: 0g; Protein: 2g; Carbs: 16g; Sugar: 8g; Fiber: 4g; Sodium: 350mg

MAPLE-CHILI SPICED ALMONDS

MAKES: 3 cups   **PREP TIME:** 5 minutes   **COOK TIME:** 15 minutes, plus 10 minutes to cool

Crunchy and perfectly sweet, these almonds make for a great snack, salad topping, or accompaniment to a cheese or charcuterie board. The chili gives them an extra special kick, but feel free to omit if you're not the spicy type. Instead, substitute ½ teaspoon cinnamon or pumpkin pie spice (for those PSL fans). These roasted nuts also make for fantastic holiday or hosting gifts—if you can resist eating them before packaging them.

Nonstick cooking spray, for coating the Dutch oven

1 tablespoon extra-virgin olive oil

2 tablespoons pure maple syrup

2 teaspoons chili powder

1½ teaspoons kosher salt

3 cups raw almonds

---

1. Preheat the oven to 325°F. Spray a Dutch oven with cooking spray.

2. In a large bowl, combine the oil, maple syrup, chili powder, and salt. Whisk until well combined.

3. Add the almonds to the bowl, and toss until well coated. Using a slotted spoon, transfer to the prepared Dutch oven, making sure they are drained of any liquid.

4. Transfer the pot to the oven, and bake, stirring halfway through the cooking time, for about 15 minutes, or until the almonds are golden. Remove from the oven. Let cool for 10 minutes. Transfer to an airtight container. The almonds will keep fresh for about 2 weeks.

✳ VARIATION TIP: This recipe calls for almonds, but you can use any raw nuts you like; it's great with a mixture of almonds, pistachios, and pecans. Peanuts are also always delicious.

Per Serving (¼ cup): Calories: 227; Total fat: 19g; Saturated fat: 2g; Protein: 7g; Carbs: 10g; Sugar: 4g; Fiber: 5g; Sodium: 304mg

CHEESE-STUFFED DATES

SERVES: 12   **PREP TIME:** 15 minutes   **COOK TIME:** 10 minutes

Stuffed dates are ideal as finger food for entertaining, holidays, or to take to a potluck. You can quickly prep these little bites ahead and store them in the refrigerator until it's time to serve. When you bite into them . . . surprise! There's a dollop of creamy, tangy, and nutty cheese filling. These dates will have everyone coming back for more.

1 cup shelled pecans	**1 (8-ounce) container mascarpone cheese**	**20 pitted medjool dates**

1. Preheat the oven to 350°F.
2. Put the pecans on a sheet pan.
3. Transfer the sheet pan to the oven, and bake for 5 to 6 minutes, or until the pecans are lightly toasted and aromatic. Remove from the oven. Let cool for 5 minutes.
4. Once cooled, put the pecans in a food processor fitted with a chopping blade, and chop until they resemble the texture of bulgur wheat or coarse sugar. Reserve ¼ cup of ground pecans in a small bowl. Pour the remaining ground pecans into a larger bowl.
5. Add the cheese, and using a spatula, mix until evenly combined.
6. Spoon the mixture into a piping bag, and securely twist and tie off the top. Snip off the pointy end to create a small opening.
7. Holding the piping bag from the top, squeeze a generous amount of the cheese mixture into the date. Close up the date, and repeat with the remaining dates.
8. Dip any exposed cheese from the stuffed dates into the reserved ground pecans to cover it up.
9. Set the dates on a serving plate. Serve immediately, or chill in the refrigerator until you are ready to serve.

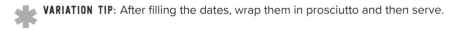 **VARIATION TIP:** After filling the dates, wrap them in prosciutto and then serve.

Per Serving: Calories: 224; Total fat: 11g; Saturated fat: 3g; Protein: 5g; Carbs: 32g; Sugar: 27g; Fiber: 4g; Sodium: 142mg

SPICY SKILLET CHICKPEAS

SERVES: 6   **PREP TIME:** 5 minutes   **COOK TIME:** 5 to 10 minutes

My daughter loves roasted chickpeas, but sometimes I'm reluctant to heat up an oven for a can's worth. Pan-roasted chickpeas yield good texture and flavor every time—the chickpeas are crispy outside and creamy inside. They're also full of protein and fiber, making for a healthy snack on their own.

---

1 (15-ounce) can chickpeas

1 tablespoon extra-virgin olive oil

1 teaspoon freshly squeezed lime juice

½ teaspoon smoked paprika

½ teaspoon ground cumin

½ teaspoon kosher salt

¼ teaspoon freshly ground black pepper

2½ tablespoons vegetable oil

---

1. Drain and rinse the chickpeas, drain well, and dry in a dish towel. Place a second towel on top, and gently roll to loosen skins, discarding as many as you can.

2. In a small bowl, mix together the olive oil, lime juice, paprika, cumin, salt, and pepper.

3. In a skillet, heat the vegetable oil over medium-high heat. Line a bowl with paper towels.

4. Carefully add the chickpeas, and cook, stirring, for 5 to 6 minutes, or until browned and crispy, being careful not to burn them. Transfer to the paper towel–lined bowl. Wipe out any remaining oil from the skillet.

5. Return the chickpeas to the skillet, and add the olive oil and lime mixture. Cook, stirring, for 20 to 30 seconds, or until well coated. Remove from the heat. Transfer to a serving bowl. Let cool for a few minutes before serving.

✳ PREP TIP: It's important to dry the chickpeas and remove the skins. They will get crisp more quickly when cooking.

Per Serving: Calories: 139; Total fat: 9g; Saturated fat: 1g; Protein: 4g; Carbs: 12g; Sugar: 2g; Fiber: 3g; Sodium: 197mg

BACON AND
CORN CHOWDER

P. 60

SOUPS AND SALADS

TOFU NOODLE BOWLS

SERVES: 4 **PREP TIME:** 5 minutes, plus 30 minutes to soak **COOK TIME:** 10 minutes

This soup, featuring rice noodles, tofu, and mushrooms, is ideal when you're in the mood for something warming but light. Unlike other soups that benefit from long simmering and taste even better after a day or so, noodle soups like this taste best when served right away.

---

8 cups water

1 cup dried shiitake
  mushrooms

¼ cup soy sauce

1 tablespoon cornstarch

1 (14-ounce) package
  medium-firm tofu, diced

1 teaspoon kosher salt

¼ teaspoon freshly ground
  black pepper

8 ounces dried rice noodles,
  cooked according to the
  package directions

---

1. In a large pot, combine the water and dried mushrooms. Let soak for 30 minutes.

2. Take the mushrooms out of the water, and cut into ⅛-inch-thick slices.

3. Return the mushrooms to the pot, and bring the water to a boil over high heat.

4. In a small bowl, stir together the soy sauce and cornstarch.

5. Add the soy sauce mixture and tofu to the pot. Return to a boil.

6. Reduce the heat to low. Simmer for 5 minutes. Season with the salt and pepper. Remove from the heat.

7. Divide the noodles among 4 bowls, ladle the broth over the noodles, and enjoy.

VARIATION TIP: Vegetables such as carrots, bok choy, spinach, onion, and garlic can be added to the soup to give it more flavor and substance. You can also serve the soup with sambal or sriracha on the side.

Per Serving: Calories: 409; Total fat: 10g; Saturated fat: 2g; Protein: 23g; Carbs: 60g; Sugar: 0g; Fiber: 5g; Sodium: 1,577mg

FRESH GAZPACHO SOUP

P. 52

FRESH GAZPACHO SOUP

(30) (DF) (NF) (VG)

SERVES: 6   **PREP TIME:** 15 minutes

Cool, refreshing gazpacho soup is a welcome break on a hot summer day. For a complete vegetarian meal, serve this soup with a crusty baguette or grilled cheese sandwiches. On days when I want to have a light dinner, I also enjoy this soup as a side to some salad, such as the Greek-Style Quinoa Salad (page 85) or Bean and Tuna Salad (page 151).

½ cup water

2 white bread slices, crusts removed

2 pounds ripe tomatoes

1 Persian cucumber, peeled and chopped

1 garlic clove, finely chopped

⅓ cup extra-virgin olive oil, plus more for garnish

2 tablespoons red wine vinegar

1 teaspoon kosher salt

½ teaspoon freshly ground black pepper

1. In a bowl, combine the water and bread. Soak for 5 minutes, then drain.

2. Put the bread, tomatoes, cucumber, garlic, oil, vinegar, salt, and pepper in a food processor or blender. Blend until completely smooth. Pour the soup into a glass container, and store in the refrigerator until completely chilled.

3. When you are ready to serve, pour the soup into a bowl, and top with a drizzle of olive oil.

✱ VARIATION TIP: You can also serve the soup topped with fresh herbs, such as basil, parsley, or thyme. I also like to add half an onion or a green or red bell pepper for some sweetness. Add these variations when blending the other ingredients in step 2.

Per Serving: Calories: 160; Total fat: 12g; Saturated fat: 2g; Protein: 3g; Carbs: 11g; Sugar: 5g; Fiber: 3g; Sodium: 441mg

SUPER EASY CHICKEN
AND TORTELLINI SOUP

P. 54

SUPER EASY CHICKEN AND TORTELLINI SOUP

SERVES: 4   **PREP TIME:** 10 minutes   **COOK TIME:** 25 to 30 minutes

This comforting tortellini soup is a nod to the classic chicken noodle soup. It's healthy, delicious comfort food with very little effort, superb for those chilly winter nights! I like to use three-cheese tortellini for this recipe, but this would also be tasty with different varieties, such as spinach and ricotta or meat-filled tortellini.

- 1 tablespoon extra-virgin olive oil
- 3 celery stalks, chopped
- 3 carrots, chopped
- 4 cups low-sodium chicken broth
- 2 cups water
- 8 ounces boneless, skinless chicken thighs
- 1 (10-ounce) package fresh cheese tortellini
- Kosher salt
- Freshly ground black pepper

---

1. In a Dutch oven, heat the oil over medium heat until shimmering.
2. Add the celery and carrots. Sauté for 3 minutes, or until starting to soften.
3. Pour in the broth and water, and add the chicken. Bring to a boil.
4. Reduce the heat to low. Simmer for 15 minutes, or until the chicken is no longer pink and its juices run clear. Transfer the chicken to a cutting board to cool.
5. Stir the tortellini into the broth, and cook for 3 to 4 minutes, or until tender.
6. Meanwhile, shred the chicken thighs, and mix the meat into the pot of soup. Remove from the heat. Season with salt and pepper. Serve.

VARIATION TIP: To make this dish vegetarian, add 10 ounces sliced mushrooms instead of the chicken, and use vegetable broth. You do not have to take the mushrooms out of the pot. Just stir in the tortellini, and finish cooking.

SUBSTITUTION TIP: I use chicken thighs in this recipe because they are more flavorful than chicken breasts—but you can use breasts if you prefer white meat.

Per Serving: Calories: 340; Total fat: 11g; Saturated fat: 4g; Protein: 21g; Carbs: 39g; Sugar: 3g; Fiber: 3g; Sodium: 436mg

TACO SOUP

SERVES: 4   **PREP TIME:** 10 minutes   **COOK TIME:** 20 minutes

Taco lovers, this soup's for you! This comforting and hearty soup is essentially beef tacos in soup form. It will quickly become a family favorite. Keep a pound of ground beef in your freezer and some basic pantry staples, and you can pull off this meal on any weeknight. Feel free to top this soup with many of the same ingredients you'd use on a taco, including guacamole, shredded cheese, or sour cream.

1 pound lean ground beef

**1 (14-ounce) can spicy
    chili beans**

4 cups beef broth

**1 (15-ounce) jar
    mild salsa**

**1 teaspoon taco
    seasoning mix**

Favorite toppings of choice

1. Put the beef in an 8-quart stockpot, and brown over medium-high heat, breaking up the meat using a spoon, for about 10 minutes, or until cooked through. Pour off and discard any fat.

2. Add the chili beans, broth, salsa, and taco seasoning. Stir to combine. Bring to a boil.

3. Reduce the heat to medium-low. Simmer for about 15 minutes. Taste, and adjust the seasoning if needed. Remove from the heat.

4. Spoon the soup into bowls, and add any toppings you like.

SUBSTITUTION TIP: To change things up, use ground chicken or turkey instead of beef. Instead of using a store-bought taco seasoning mix, you can use 1 teaspoon ground cumin, ½ teaspoon kosher salt, and ½ teaspoon freshly ground black pepper.

Per Serving: Calories: 325; Total fat: 12g; Saturated fat: 5g; Protein: 29g; Carbs: 24g; Sugar: 9g; Fiber: 6g; Sodium: 1,132mg

EASY BROWN LENTIL SOUP

SERVES: 6   **PREP TIME:** 25 minutes   **COOK TIME:** 1 hour 20 minutes

When the cold weather sets in, there's nothing like a big bowl of lentil soup to warm you up. This soup is on the thicker side—you can thin it out with a little coconut milk to give it a richer flavor or add a little more water or vegetable broth if you prefer. Serve this with croutons or crispy pita chips.

---

10 cups water

2 cups dried brown lentils, picked over and rinsed

2 teaspoons kosher salt, divided

¼ cup long-grain rice, rinsed

3 tablespoons extra-virgin olive oil

1 large onion, chopped

2 medium potatoes, peeled and cut into ¼-inch pieces

1 teaspoon ground cumin

½ teaspoon freshly ground black pepper

---

1. In a large pot, combine the water, lentils, and 1 teaspoon of salt. Bring to a simmer over medium heat. Cook, stirring occasionally, for 30 minutes.

2. Add the rice, cover, and continue to simmer, stirring occasionally, for another 30 minutes. Remove from the heat. Using a handheld immersion blender, blend for 1 to 2 minutes, or until smooth.

3. Return the pot to the stove over low heat.

4. In a small skillet, combine the oil and onion. Cook over medium heat for 5 minutes, or until the onion is golden brown. Remove from the heat.

5. To the pot, add the onion, potatoes, remaining 1 teaspoon of salt, cumin, and pepper. Stir, and cook for 10 to 15 minutes, or until the potatoes have thoroughly cooked. Remove from the heat. Serve warm.

✳ VARIATION TIP: When serving, garnish the bowl with a sprinkle of freshly chopped parsley. If you're not following a vegan or vegetarian diet, you can easily make this delicious soup even heartier by adding cooked mini meatballs and chopped carrots.

Per Serving: Calories: 379; Total fat: 8g; Saturated fat: 1g; Protein: 18g; Carbs: 61g; Sugar: 3g; Fiber: 9g; Sodium: 398mg

TUSCAN BEAN SOUP

SERVES: 4 **PREP TIME:** 5 minutes **COOK TIME:** 20 minutes

Healthy, wholesome, and satisfying, this Italian-style bean soup has it all: flavorful sausage, delightful cannellini beans, and heart-healthy spinach. It'll really have you saying, "Buon appetito!" when you dig in. An added bonus? Leftovers reheat nicely the next day. Garnish this filling soup with freshly grated parmesan cheese for an authentic boost of flavor.

1 tablespoon extra-virgin olive oil

1 onion, diced

8 ounces turkey or chicken sausage, casing removed

4 cups low-sodium chicken broth

½ teaspoon kosher salt, plus more for seasoning

½ teaspoon freshly ground black pepper, plus more for seasoning

1 (15-ounce) can cannellini beans, drained and rinsed

8 ounces fresh spinach

1. In a large stockpot, warm the oil over medium heat.

2. Add the onion and sausage. Sauté, using a spoon to break up the sausage, for 3 to 4 minutes, or until the meat is no longer pink.

3. Add the broth, salt, and pepper. Stir to combine.

4. Increase the heat to medium-high. Bring the soup to a boil. Add the beans and spinach.

5. Reduce the heat to medium-low. Simmer for 4 to 5 minutes, or until the soup has cooked through. Remove from the heat. Taste, and adjust the seasoning with salt and pepper if needed.

SUBSTITUTION TIP: For a vegetarian soup, do not add the sausage. Instead, add 1 (14-ounce) can diced tomatoes with their juices, and substitute vegetable broth for chicken broth.

Per Serving: Calories: 226; Total fat: 9g; Saturated fat: 2g; Protein: 18g; Carbs: 20g; Sugar: 2g; Fiber: 7g; Sodium: 674mg

THAI-INSPIRED SWEET POTATO CURRY SOUP

SERVES: 4 **PREP TIME:** 15 minutes **COOK TIME:** 30 to 35 minutes

Thai curry paste is a versatile and mouthwatering base for a variety of Thai dishes. It's also a nice condiment to keep in your pantry or refrigerator to add complexity to soups, stews, and sauces. Not all curry pastes are created equal—some are more pungent and spicier than others—so be sure to try a few different brands to find one you like.

---

2 tablespoons vegetable oil

2 tablespoons Thai red curry paste or massaman curry paste

2 cups diced peeled sweet potatoes

8 ounces boneless, skinless chicken breast, cut into small pieces

2 small broccoli heads, florets separated and stems chopped

1 (14-ounce) can coconut milk

2 cups water

Fresh cilantro, for garnish (optional)

---

1. In a stockpot, heat the oil over medium-high heat until shimmering.
2. Add the curry paste, and cook, stirring, for 1 minute.
3. Add the sweet potatoes, chicken, and broccoli. Cook for 8 minutes.
4. Add the coconut milk and water. Whisk until combined. Bring just to a boil.
5. Reduce the heat to a gentle simmer. Cover, and cook, stirring occasionally, for about 20 minutes. Remove from the heat.
6. Ladle the soup into bowls. Garnish with the cilantro (if using), and serve.

✱ COOKING TIP: You can also make this soup in a slow cooker. Combine all the ingredients except the cilantro in a slow cooker, and cook on high for 3 hours. Then finish the soup as in step 6.

Per Serving: Calories: 492; Total fat: 31g; Saturated fat: 20g; Protein: 25g; Carbs: 38g; Sugar: 8g; Fiber: 12g; Sodium: 190mg

BACON AND CORN CHOWDER

SERVES: 4   **PREP TIME:** 10 minutes   **COOK TIME:** 40 minutes

Thanks to the cream-style canned corn, you can cozy up to a bowl of this corn chowder any time of the year. Despite its name, cream-style corn gets its creaminess from pulped corn kernels. You'll want to make a big pot of this so you can have the leftovers for lunch the next day.

---

1 cup diced peeled russet
  potatoes
Kosher salt
4 bacon slices, diced

1 medium onion, diced
1 (14-ounce) can
  cream-style corn

3 cups whole milk
Freshly ground black pepper

---

1. Put the potatoes in a medium pot, and add water to cover by 2 inches. Season with salt. Bring to a boil over high heat. Cook for about 12 minutes, or until the potatoes are soft. Remove from the heat. Drain in a colander.

2. Rinse out the pot, and return to the stove over medium heat. Add the bacon, and cook for 5 minutes.

3. Add the onion, and cook for 5 more minutes.

4. Carefully drain off the bacon fat, leaving the bacon and onion in the pot.

5. Add the cream-style corn and milk. Heat over medium heat for about 10 minutes, or until hot, but do not let boil.

6. Add the cooked potatoes, and cook for 2 minutes to let them absorb some of the flavor. Remove from the heat. Season with salt and pepper. Serve.

VARIATION TIP: Add 1 (4-ounce) can diced green chiles for Southwestern flavors and a little heat.

Per Serving: Calories: 278; Total fat: 10g; Saturated fat: 5g; Protein: 13g; Carbs: 36g; Sugar: 14g; Fiber: 2g; Sodium: 573mg

SMOKY SPLIT PEA SOUP WITH BACON

SERVES: 4 **PREP TIME:** 15 minutes **COOK TIME:** 1 hour 30 minutes

Split peas are cooked down with bacon and vegetables to create a thick, velvety, stick-to-your-ribs soup that's excellent served with slices of toasted bread or Nectarine-Tomato Bruschetta (page 34). Try using smoked ham hock or smoked turkey legs in place of the bacon to impart more flavor into the soup.

---

6 bacon slices, chopped

1 medium onion, chopped

2 large carrots, chopped

1 pound dried split peas

8 cups low-sodium chicken broth

2 cups water

Kosher salt

Freshly ground black pepper

---

1. Put the bacon in a large Dutch oven, and cook over medium-high heat for 10 minutes, or until crispy. If there are more than a few tablespoons of bacon fat in the Dutch oven, pour some off, leaving just a few spoonfuls.

2. Add the onion and carrots. Sauté for 5 minutes, or until soft.

3. Add the split peas, broth, and water. Cover, and bring to a boil.

4. Reduce the heat to a simmer. Cook, stirring occasionally, for about 1 hour 10 minutes, or until the split peas are soft. The soup can be cooked longer if you like a creamier consistency. Remove from the heat. Season with salt and pepper before serving.

COOKING TIP: This soup may also be cooked a day ahead and refrigerated because its flavor and texture develop nicely overnight.

Per Serving: Calories: 511; Total fat: 8g; Saturated fat: 2g; Protein: 34g; Carbs: 80g; Sugar: 12g; Fiber: 31g; Sodium: 398mg

ARUGULA-WATERMELON SALAD

(30) (GF) (NF) (OP) (V)

SERVES: 2 **PREP TIME:** 5 minutes

Jazz up any picnic or backyard barbecue with this colorful salad. It's a tasty combination of juicy watermelon, peppery arugula, tangy goat cheese, and creamy avocado, with a touch of zing from the balsamic vinegar to tie all the flavors together. If you've never tried watermelon in a savory dish, give this recipe a try.

---

4 cups arugula

2 tablespoons extra-virgin olive oil

½ cup diced watermelon

¼ cup goat cheese, crumbled

¼ ripe avocado, pitted, peeled, and sliced

⅛ teaspoon kosher salt (optional)

1 tablespoon balsamic vinegar

---

1. In a bowl, toss together the arugula and oil.

2. Add the watermelon, cheese, avocado, and salt (if using). Toss lightly.

3. Drizzle the vinegar on top. Serve immediately.

✳ SUBSTITUTION TIP: You can use feta instead of goat cheese. Strawberries can replace watermelon, and if you run out of arugula, try baby spinach.

Per Serving: Calories: 226; Total fat: 21g; Saturated fat: 5g; Protein: 4g; Carbs: 8g; Sugar: 4g; Fiber: 3g; Sodium: 80mg

SOBA NOODLE SALAD

SERVES: 2   **PREP TIME:** 10 minutes

Crunchy vegetables and nutty buckwheat noodles combine to make this a scrumptious vegan dish. You can also add some grilled or sautéed shrimp, chicken, or tofu for a more substantial meal. Whole-wheat spaghetti noodles can be a good stand-in, but I recommend soba if you can find it. To add a little color to the final salad, garnish it with black and white sesame seeds and thinly sliced scallions.

---

2 cups cooked soba noodles (follow the package directions), rinsed in cold water

½ cup grated carrot
½ cup thinly sliced bok choy
½ cup thinly sliced red bell pepper

¼ cup sesame-ginger dressing

---

1. In a medium bowl, toss together the noodles, carrot, bok choy, and bell pepper.

2. Add the dressing, and toss to coat.

SUBSTITUTION TIP: If you can't find bok choy at the grocery store, you can replace it with any kind of cabbage if it's very thinly sliced.

RECIPE TIP: To make the sesame-ginger dressing, whisk together 1 tablespoon tahini, 1 tablespoon rice vinegar, 1 tablespoon low-sodium soy sauce, 1 teaspoon sesame oil, ½ teaspoon grated ginger, and ½ teaspoon honey until smooth.

Per Serving: Calories: 273; Total fat: 14g; Saturated fat: 2g; Protein: 7g; Carbs: 32g; Sugar: 6g; Fiber: 2g; Sodium: 399mg

ORANGE AND RED ONION SALAD

(30) (DF) (GF) (NF) (VG)

SERVES: 4 **PREP TIME:** 15 minutes

This sweet, tart, and crunchy salad featuring oranges, red onion, and briny olives is almost too pretty to eat. If you'd like, arrange a bed of mixed greens or baby spinach on a platter, and arrange the salad on top of it. I like to serve this to guests coming over for lunch, especially to bust those winter blues in colder weather.

---

3 or 4 tablespoons
    extra-virgin olive oil
Juice of 1 lemon

Kosher salt
Freshly ground black pepper
4 large oranges

1 large red onion, thinly sliced
¼ cup pitted olives of choice

---

1. To make the vinaigrette, in a small bowl, combine the oil and lemon juice. Season well with salt and pepper. Using a fork, mix well.

2. Thoroughly peel the oranges, and remove all the white pith. Cut the oranges into ⅛-inch-thick slices, and decoratively arrange on a platter.

3. Top with the onion, and sprinkle with the olives.

4. Dress the salad with the vinaigrette. Season with salt and pepper if desired.

SUBSTITUTION TIP: If you happen to have grapefruits on hand as opposed to oranges, feel free to substitute. Any citrus fruit will do for this citrus salad.

Per Serving: Calories: 185; Total fat: 11g; Saturated fat: 2g; Protein: 2g; Carbs: 22g; Sugar: 14g; Fiber: 4g; Sodium: 104mg

ZESTY SPINACH SALAD

(30) (DF) (GF) (NF) (VG)

SERVES: 4   **PREP TIME:** 10 minutes

Spinach, tomato, and red onion are featured in this simple yet flavorful salad, adding a burst of color and nutrition to the plate. It's perfect to serve with everyday meals and especially pairs well with a rich stew or pasta dish, like Country-Style Pork Ragù (page 165) and Quick Shrimp Fettuccine (page 79). Spinach can wilt very quickly, so it's best to dress the salad right before serving.

½ teaspoon grated lemon zest	¼ cup extra-virgin olive oil	1 large ripe tomato, cut into ¼-inch dice
3 tablespoons balsamic vinegar	½ teaspoon kosher salt	1 medium red onion, cut into long slivers
	1 pound baby spinach, washed and stemmed	

1. To make the dressing, in a small bowl, whisk together the lemon zest, vinegar, oil, and salt.

2. In a large bowl, combine the spinach, tomato, and onion.

3. Pour the dressing over the salad, and lightly toss to coat.

✻ VARIATION TIP: For a crunchy topping, add ⅓ cup toasted pine nuts. Simply toast the pine nuts in a small skillet over medium-low heat for about 3 minutes, or until golden brown.

Per Serving: Calories: 175; Total fat: 14g; Saturated fat: 2g; Protein: 4g; Carbs: 11g; Sugar: 5g; Fiber: 4g; Sodium: 387mg

STRAWBERRY-SPINACH
SALAD

P. 68

STRAWBERRY-SPINACH SALAD

SERVES: 2   **PREP TIME:** 10 minutes

This salad is a festive way to celebrate strawberry season. I like Gorgonzola blue cheese crumbles because they have the best tangy flavor to pair with sweet strawberries. If blue cheese is a little too intense, you can replace it with feta, goat cheese, or even diced avocado for a vegan version.

---

1 tablespoon balsamic vinegar
½ cup extra-virgin olive oil
Kosher salt
Freshly ground black pepper

1 (10-ounce) package fresh baby spinach, washed, dried, and torn into pieces
2 cups sliced strawberries

¼ cup blanched, slivered almonds
½ cup crumbled blue cheese

---

1. To make the dressing, in a small bowl, mix together the vinegar and oil. Season with salt and pepper.

2. Put the spinach in a large bowl, and add the dressing, strawberries, and almonds. Gently toss to coat.

3. Sprinkle with the blue cheese before serving.

VARIATION TIP: You could use coarsely chopped walnuts or pecans instead of (or in addition to) the almonds.

Per Serving: Calories: 767; Total fat: 71g; Saturated fat: 14g; Protein: 15g; Carbs: 23g; Sugar: 11g; Fiber: 8g; Sodium: 581mg

ROASTED RED PEPPER SALAD

SERVES: 4   **PREP TIME:** 5 minutes   **COOK TIME:** 30 minutes

Roasted red peppers arranged on a platter and drizzled with olive oil and vinegar makes for one simple yet elegant salad. This is less conventional than your typical mixed greens salad, but it has the potential to become your new go-to. Try using a combination of red, orange, and yellow bell peppers for a colorful twist.

6 long red peppers

2 tablespoons extra-virgin olive oil

1 tablespoon white wine vinegar

¼ teaspoon kosher salt, plus more for seasoning

1 tablespoon fresh parsley, chopped

1. Set the oven to broil. Line a sheet pan with parchment paper.

2. Arrange the peppers in a single layer, skin-side up, on the prepared sheet pan.

3. Transfer the sheet pan to the oven, and broil the peppers on one side for about 5 minutes, or until the skin starts bubbling.

4. Flip the peppers, and broil on the other side. Keep turning until all sides of the peppers are brown and the skin lifts up from the flesh. This should take 15 to 20 minutes, depending on your oven. Remove from the oven. Cover the sheet pan with a kitchen towel. Let rest for 10 minutes.

5. Peel the skin off the peppers, and lay the peppers flat on a serving plate.

6. Drizzle with the oil and vinegar. Season with the salt. Using clean hands, gently toss the peppers so the dressing is evenly applied.

7. Sprinkle the peppers with a little salt and the parsley. Serve immediately, or refrigerate for about 15 minutes to cool further.

SUBSTITUTION TIP: If you cannot find any long red peppers, you can use red bell peppers.

COOKING TIP: If you have a grill, you can grill the peppers instead of broiling them; the taste is even better if you have a charcoal grill.

Per Serving: Calories: 137; Total fat: 8g; Saturated fat: 1g; Protein: 2g; Carbs: 15g; Sugar: 10g; Fiber: 5g; Sodium: 156mg

GREEK-STYLE
QUINOA SALAD

P. 85

5

PASTA AND GRAINS

LEMON ORZO WITH FRESH HERBS

SERVES: 4 **PREP TIME:** 10 minutes **COOK TIME:** 10 to 15 minutes

We love to cook with orzo around here. It's a great change from rice, cooks in half the time, and is a delicious canvas for a host of flavors, such as fresh herbs and lemon. Toss with some tofu, chicken, or shrimp for a more protein-packed meal.

2 cups orzo

½ cup fresh parsley, finely chopped

½ cup fresh basil leaves, finely chopped

2 tablespoons grated lemon zest

½ cup extra-virgin olive oil

⅓ cup freshly squeezed lemon juice

1 teaspoon kosher salt

½ teaspoon freshly ground black pepper

1. Bring a large pot of water to a boil over high heat.

2. Add the orzo, and cook for 7 minutes. Remove from the heat. Drain in a colander, and rinse with cold water. Let the orzo sit in the colander to completely drain and cool.

3. In a large bowl, combine the orzo, parsley, basil, and lemon zest.

4. To make the dressing, in a small bowl, whisk together the oil, lemon juice, salt, and pepper.

5. Add the dressing to the orzo, and toss together. Serve at room temperature or chilled.

VARIATION TIP: Add asparagus stalks cut into bite-size pieces for a more substantial vegetarian dish.

Per Serving: Calories: 573; Total fat: 28g; Saturated fat: 4g; Protein: 11g; Carbs: 69g; Sugar: 1g; Fiber: 5g; Sodium: 595mg

ORECCHIETTE WITH BROCCOLI RABE AND SAUSAGE

SERVES: 4 **PREP TIME:** 10 minutes **COOK TIME:** 20 to 25 minutes

Orecchiette, or pasta shaped like little ears, is the classic choice for this dish. Its cup-like shape is ideal for catching every bit of the sausage and broccoli rabe. Sweet Italian sausage balances out the slightly bitter flavor of the greens, but hot sausage also works if you prefer the spiciness.

2 bunches broccoli rabe	**¼ cup extra-virgin olive oil,**	**4 to 6 Italian sausages,**
Kosher salt	**plus more for drizzling**	**casings removed**
12 ounces orecchiette	**½ small onion, finely chopped**	

1. Trim the broccoli rabe by removing and discarding the lower ends and lower leaves, keeping just the florets.

2. Bring a large pot of salted water to a boil.

3. Add the florets, and boil for 5 to 6 minutes. Using kitchen tongs, remove the florets from the boiling water, and set aside.

4. Add the orecchiette to the same water, and cook for 2 minutes less than directed on the package. Remove from the heat. Drain in a colander.

5. Meanwhile, in a large sauté pan, heat the oil over medium-high heat.

6. Add the onion and sausages. Break the sausage up to resemble ground meat. Sauté for 7 to 8 minutes.

7. Add the florets, and stir to coat with the oil. Cook for 1 minute.

8. Add the orecchiette, and cook for 2 minutes. Remove from the heat. Serve hot, and drizzle with more oil if desired.

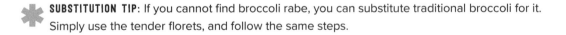

SUBSTITUTION TIP: If you cannot find broccoli rabe, you can substitute traditional broccoli for it. Simply use the tender florets, and follow the same steps.

Per Serving: Calories: 747; Total fat: 37g; Saturated fat: 10g; Protein: 29g; Carbs: 72g; Sugar: 4g; Fiber: 9g; Sodium: 650mg

PASTA CARBONARA

SERVES: 4   **PREP TIME:** 10 minutes   **COOK TIME:** 15 minutes

As far as a good dish for a cold day goes, this one hits the spot. The rich and creamy sauce makes this hearty pasta a family favorite. Plus, it's ready in less than half an hour. A bright, green salad, such as Zesty Spinach Salad (page 66), pairs well with this pasta dish.

Kosher salt

12 ounces spaghetti

3 large eggs

¼ cup grated Pecorino Romano cheese, plus more for sprinkling

6 ounces diced pancetta, or 6 ounces thick-cut bacon, diced

3 tablespoons extra-virgin olive oil

1. Bring a large pot of salted water to a boil over high heat.
2. Add the spaghetti, and cook for 2 minutes less than directed on the package. Remove from the heat. Drain in a colander.
3. In a small bowl, whisk together the eggs and cheese.
4. While the spaghetti is cooking, put the pancetta in a large sauté pan, and cook over medium heat for 6 to 7 minutes, or until crisp and all the fat has rendered.
5. Add the pasta and oil. Toss to combine.
6. Reduce the heat to low. Add the egg and cheese mixture, stirring constantly to avoid scrambling the eggs. Cook for 1 minute, all the while stirring. Remove from the heat.
7. Plate the pasta, and top with additional cheese.

SUBSTITUTION TIP: Pecorino Romano is a hard sheep cheese with a salty, tangy flavor. If you find the flavor too strong, replace with the milder Parmigiano-Reggiano.

Per Serving: Calories: 663; Total fat: 34g; Saturated fat: 10g; Protein: 23g; Carbs: 64g; Sugar: 3g; Fiber: 3g; Sodium: 481mg

CACIO E PEPE WITH FRESH HERBS

SERVES: 6 **PREP TIME:** 10 minutes **COOK TIME:** 20 minutes

I love this cacio e pepe recipe because it is humble yet so satisfying. It basically uses pasta water, cheese, and butter to create a rich sauce that is truly indulgent and packs a ton of flavor. It comes together in a flash, which makes it my top meal for weeknight dinners.

Kosher salt

1 (16-ounce) box thick spaghetti

1 teaspoon freshly ground black pepper

4 tablespoons (½ stick) unsalted butter

½ cup freshly grated parmesan cheese, plus more for serving

2 tablespoons extra-virgin olive oil

Small handful chopped fresh basil or parsley, for serving

1. Fill a Dutch oven with salted water, and bring to a boil over high heat.

2. Add the spaghetti, and cook for 9 minutes, or until al dente. Reserve 1 cup of the cooking water, then drain the spaghetti in a colander.

3. Reduce the heat to medium. Add the pepper to the Dutch oven, and toast for 30 seconds.

4. Add the butter, and cook for 1 to 2 minutes, or until melted.

5. Add the reserved cooking water and the cheese. Mix well so the cheese melts into the cooking water.

6. Add the spaghetti, and toss vigorously until well coated with the cheese sauce.

7. Mix in the oil. Season with salt. Remove from the heat.

8. Sprinkle and toss with the fresh herbs right before serving. Serve with additional cheese if desired.

PREP TIP: Make sure to use freshly ground pepper and freshly grated parmesan cheese for this recipe. It really makes a difference.

Per Serving: Calories: 425; Total fat: 16g; Saturated fat: 7g; Protein: 12g; Carbs: 58g; Sugar: 2g; Fiber: 3g; Sodium: 159mg

ANGEL HAIR PASTA WITH GARLIC SPINACH

SERVES: 6   **PREP TIME:** 5 minutes   **COOK TIME:** 10 minutes

Fragrant garlic and bright, fresh spinach are the stars in this recipe. It's almost too simple, but then, who says food has to be complicated to be crave-worthy? A pinch of red pepper flakes stirred into the olive oil helps kick the heat up a notch.

---

1 (16-ounce) box angel hair pasta

⅓ cup extra-virgin olive oil

4 or 5 garlic cloves, minced

½ teaspoon red pepper flakes

2 cups baby spinach, chopped

Kosher salt

Freshly ground black pepper

---

1. Cook the pasta according to the package directions. Remove from the heat. Drain in a colander well. Return to the pot.

2. In a small skillet, heat the oil over medium heat.

3. Add the garlic and red pepper flakes. Cook, stirring once or twice, for 1 to 2 minutes, or until the garlic is fragrant but not browned. Remove from the heat. Pour over the pasta in the pot, and toss well.

4. Add the spinach, and toss again. Season with salt and pepper. Serve.

VARIATION TIP: For a cheesy version of this pasta, add ¼ cup freshly grated romano cheese at the same time as the spinach.

Per Serving: Calories: 391; Total fat: 13g; Saturated fat: 2g; Protein: 10g; Carbs: 57g; Sugar: 2g; Fiber: 3g; Sodium: 54mg

PESTO CHICKEN AND BROCCOLI WITH PENNE AND SUN-DRIED TOMATOES

SERVES: 6   **PREP TIME:** 10 minutes   **COOK TIME:** 30 minutes

When everyone is arriving home after a long day of work or school, hungry and tired, asking "What's for dinner?"—this dish is your answer. This dinner is guaranteed to satisfy even the pickiest of palates. Finish off the meal with some warm Peanut Butter Cookies (page 207) that will be just as quick and easy to make as dinner.

1 (16-ounce) box penne

12 ounces broccoli florets

2 tablespoons extra-virgin olive oil

1 pound boneless, skinless chicken breasts, chopped into bite-size pieces

⅓ cup sun-dried tomatoes

⅓ cup pesto

Grated parmesan cheese, for serving (optional)

1. Fill a Dutch oven with water, and bring to a boil over medium-high heat.

2. Add the penne, and cook for about 10 minutes, or until al dente (or follow the package directions). During the last 3 minutes of cooking, add the broccoli. Reserve 1 cup of the cooking water, then drain the penne and broccoli in a colander. Keep warm.

3. Reduce the heat to medium. Add the oil to the pot, and stir in the chicken. Cook for about 7 minutes, or until the chicken has browned.

4. Add the sun-dried tomatoes, pesto, and reserved cooking water. Stir well, and cook for a few minutes to bring to a simmer.

5. Add the penne and broccoli. Toss well, and cook, stirring occasionally, for a few minutes, or until the sauce starts to thicken. Remove from the heat. Transfer to a large serving bowl.

6. Sprinkle with the cheese (if using) before serving.

✳ PREP TIP: To save time, you can substitute frozen broccoli for fresh. Just add it in step 2, and cook it with the sauce for a few extra minutes.

Per Serving: Calories: 506; Total fat: 15g; Saturated fat: 2g; Protein: 31g; Carbs: 62g; Sugar: 4g; Fiber: 4g; Sodium: 205mg

QUICK SHRIMP FETTUCCINE

SERVES: 4 **PREP TIME:** 10 minutes **COOK TIME:** 15 minutes

This shrimp pasta, reminiscent of the flavors of shrimp scampi, is one of my favorite weeknight dinners whenever I'm in the mood for seafood. The aromatic garlic and bright lemon pair wonderfully with the shrimp. Serve this with a tossed salad, such as Strawberry-Spinach Salad (page 68), or crusty bread.

½ teaspoon kosher salt, plus more for boiling the fettuccine

8 ounces fettuccine

¼ cup extra-virgin olive oil

3 garlic cloves, minced

1 pound large (21/25 count per pound) shrimp, peeled and deveined

⅓ cup freshly squeezed lemon juice

1 tablespoon grated lemon zest

½ teaspoon freshly ground black pepper

1. Bring a large pot of salted water to a boil over high heat.

2. Add the fettuccine, and cook for 8 minutes, or until al dente. Remove from the heat. Reserve ½ cup of the cooking water, then drain the fettuccine in a colander.

3. Meanwhile, in a large saucepan, combine the oil and garlic. Cook over medium heat for 1 minute.

4. Add the shrimp, and cook for 3 minutes per side. Remove the shrimp from the pan, and set aside.

5. Add the lemon juice, lemon zest, salt, and pepper.

6. Add the reserved cooking water, and stir everything together.

7. Add the fettuccine, and toss together to evenly coat. Remove from the heat. Transfer to a serving dish.

8. Top with the cooked shrimp. Serve warm.

VARIATION TIP: You can add 1 cup heavy cream to the sauce in the pan and let it simmer for 2 minutes. Top it off with 2 tablespoons freshly chopped basil for a creamy texture and more flavor.

Per Serving: Calories: 418; Total fat: 16g; Saturated fat: 2g; Protein: 23g; Carbs: 46g; Sugar: 2g; Fiber: 2g; Sodium: 937mg

CREAMY TORTELLINI WITH PEAS AND CRISPY PROSCIUTTO

SERVES: 4 **PREP TIME:** 5 minutes **COOK TIME:** 25 minutes

File this pasta recipe in the "easy decadence" section of your recipe archive, thanks to the fresh tortellini that cooks in no time and rich sauce mixed with prosciutto. When you buy fresh pasta, be sure to prepare it within a day or two, or else it dries up and doesn't taste as fresh.

---

1 (10-ounce) package fresh
  cheese tortellini

2 tablespoons extra-virgin
  olive oil

3 ounces prosciutto, chopped

1½ cups frozen peas

½ cup half-and-half

3 tablespoons chopped fresh
  basil leaves, plus more
  for garnish

Kosher salt

Freshly ground black pepper

---

1. Fill a Dutch oven three-quarters full of water, and bring to a boil over high heat.
2. Reduce the heat to medium. Add the tortellini, and cook for 6 minutes, or until al dente (or follow the package directions). Drain in a colander, and keep warm.
3. In the Dutch oven, heat the oil over medium heat. Line a plate with paper towels.
4. Add the prosciutto, and cook for about 5 minutes, or until crispy. Using a slotted spoon, transfer to the prepared plate.
5. Add the peas to the Dutch oven, and cook for 5 minutes, or until tender.
6. Reduce the heat to low. Add the tortellini, half-and-half, and basil. Stir to combine. Cook for a few minutes, or until the sauce slightly thickens. Taste, and season with salt and pepper. Remove from the heat. Transfer to a big bowl.
7. Add the prosciutto, and toss.
8. Serve the pasta garnished with basil.

VARIATION TIP: Some grocery stores sell a variety of fresh tortellini—cheese-filled as well as pesto and spinach. Try a different flavor every time and then choose your favorite, or mix them together in the same dish to add color and variety.

Per Serving: Calories: 396; Total fat: 17g; Saturated fat: 6g; Protein: 17g; Carbs: 43g; Sugar: 5g; Fiber: 4g; Sodium: 585mg

CHEESY SPINACH ZITI BAKE

(NF)

SERVES: 6 **PREP TIME:** 5 minutes **COOK TIME:** 45 minutes

When I was first learning to cook, baked ziti was a favorite. It's a comforting combination of pasta, marinara sauce, ricotta cheese, and mozzarella cheese that's straightforward to assemble. This one-pot version makes it even easier with a store-bought sauce that gets heated on the stovetop and then finished in the oven.

---

1 (16-ounce) box ziti

3 cups marinara sauce

1 (10-ounce) package frozen chopped spinach, thawed

Kosher salt

Freshly ground black pepper

2 cups ricotta cheese

3 cups shredded mozzarella cheese, divided

---

1. Preheat the oven to 350°F.

2. Fill a Dutch oven with water, and bring to a boil over high heat.

3. Add the ziti, and cook until al dente, according to the package directions. Drain in a colander, and keep warm.

4. Reduce the heat to medium-high. In the Dutch oven, heat the marinara sauce.

5. Add the spinach, and cook for 10 minutes, or until the mixture comes to a simmer. Season with salt and pepper. Remove from the heat.

6. Add the ziti, and mix in the ricotta cheese and 2 cups of mozzarella cheese. Make sure everything is well mixed. Sprinkle the remaining 1 cup of mozzarella cheese on top.

7. Cover the pot, transfer to the oven, and bake for about 20 minutes, or until the pasta is bubbling.

8. Remove the lid, and bake for 5 more minutes, or until the cheese melts and starts to turn golden. Remove from the oven. Let cool slightly before serving.

✳ COOKING TIP: If you are taking this pasta dish to a potluck dinner, prepare the recipe through step 6, just before you add the mozzarella on top. Transfer everything to a 9-by-13-inch disposable aluminum pan, sprinkle on the mozzarella, and cover the pan with aluminum foil. When you get there, bake the dish for 20 minutes at 350°F, then remove the foil, and bake for 5 more minutes.

Per Serving: Calories: 635; Total fat: 25g; Saturated fat: 14g; Protein: 35g; Carbs: 68g; Sugar: 7g; Fiber: 6g; Sodium: 499mg

MEATY BAKED PENNE

(NF)

SERVES: 8   **PREP TIME:** 10 minutes   **COOK TIME:** 40 to 45 minutes

A good baked pasta dish like this one, made with ground beef, mozzarella, and spinach, is always a crowd-pleaser and makes entertaining or weeknight cooking a cakewalk. Finishing this recipe off with fresh herbs can add a nice dimension to the dish. Try sprinkling it with chopped fresh parsley or basil.

1 (16-ounce) box penne
1 pound lean ground beef
1 teaspoon kosher salt

1 (25-ounce) jar
    marinara sauce
1 (1-pound) bag baby
    spinach, washed

3 cups shredded mozzarella
    cheese, divided

1. Bring a large pot of salted water to a boil over high heat.

2. Add the penne, and cook for 7 minutes. Remove from the heat. Reserve 2 cups of the cooking water, then drain the penne in a colander.

3. Preheat the oven to 350°F.

4. While the penne cooks, put the beef in a large saucepan. Season with the salt. Cook over medium heat for about 5 minutes, or until browned.

5. Stir in the marinara sauce and reserved cooking water and spinach. Simmer for 5 minutes.

6. To assemble, put the penne in a 9-by-13-inch baking dish, and pour the pasta sauce over it.

7. Stir in 1½ cups of cheese. Cover the dish with aluminum foil.

8. Transfer the baking dish to the oven, and bake for 20 minutes.

9. Remove the foil. Top with the remaining 1½ cups of cheese, and bake for 10 minutes. Remove from the oven. Serve warm.

✳ **VARIATION TIP:** For more vegetables, you can add sautéed mushrooms or cooked chopped onions after step 6.

Per Serving: Calories: 470; Total fat: 16g; Saturated fat: 8g; Protein: 31g; Carbs: 50g; Sugar: 5g; Fiber: 4g; Sodium: 649mg

➡️

PASTA E FAGIOLI

P. 84

PASTA E FAGIOLI

SERVES: 4   **PREP TIME:** 10 minutes   **COOK TIME:** 15 to 20 minutes

Pasta e fagioli is a traditional Italian soup that translates to "pasta and beans." True to its name, here we use hearty doses of white beans, rotini, and vegetables. If this cozy bowl of soup isn't enough, you can "fare la scarpetta" (clean the bowl with bread) with some garlic bread, soaking up every last glorious drop.

---

8 ounces rotini

2 tablespoons extra-virgin olive oil

1 bunch kale, stemmed and chopped

1 (15-ounce) can diced tomatoes, drained

1 (15-ounce) can white beans, drained and rinsed

1 teaspoon dried oregano

Kosher salt

Freshly ground black pepper

---

1. Fill a large saucepan with water. Bring to a boil over high heat.

2. Add the rotini, and cook until al dente, according to the package directions. Remove from the heat. Reserve about ½ cup of the cooking water, then drain the rotini in a colander.

3. While the rotini cooks, in a large skillet, heat the oil over medium-high heat.

4. Add the kale, and sauté for 4 to 6 minutes, or until wilted.

5. Add the tomatoes and beans. Cook for 3 to 5 minutes, or until heated through and the tomatoes release some of their water. Season with the oregano, salt, and pepper.

6. Stir in the rotini and ¼ cup of the reserved cooking water. Cook, stirring continuously, for 1 minute, or until heated through. If desired, add the remaining ¼ cup of the reserved cooking water to create a thinner soup. Remove from the heat.

VARIATION TIP: To boost the flavor in this dish, add 2 tablespoons vegan nutritional yeast or shredded parmesan cheese to each serving.

Per Serving: Calories: 391; Total fat: 8g; Saturated fat: 1g; Protein: 15g; Carbs: 65g; Sugar: 5g; Fiber: 12g; Sodium: 172mg

GREEK-STYLE QUINOA SALAD

(DF) (GF) (NF) (VG)

SERVES: 6   **PREP TIME:** 5 minutes   **COOK TIME:** 25 minutes, plus time to cool

This bright and colorful quinoa salad has a Greek flair, thanks to the tomatoes, cucumber, olives, and lemon dressing. It works equally well as a vegan main dish salad or side dish to grilled fish or chicken, such as Sun-Dried Tomato Pesto Snapper (page 140) and Pan Chicken with Tomatoes (page 113).

FOR THE DRESSING
¼ cup extra-virgin olive oil
Juice of ½ large lemon
½ teaspoon kosher salt

FOR THE QUINOA
2 cups quinoa,
    thoroughly rinsed
4 cups water

1¼ cups cherry tomatoes,
    quartered
½ English cucumber, diced
½ cup Kalamata olives, pitted
    and chopped

1. **To make the dressing:** In a bowl, whisk together the oil, lemon juice, and salt.
2. **To make the quinoa:** In a medium saucepan, combine the quinoa and water. Bring to a boil over high heat.
3. Reduce the heat to low. Cover, and simmer for 15 minutes, or until the water has been absorbed. Remove from the heat.
4. Remove the lid. Using a fork, fluff the quinoa. Cover, and let rest for about 5 minutes. Transfer to a large wooden or glass salad bowl. Let cool.
5. Once the quinoa has cooled to room temperature, add the tomatoes, cucumber, and olives. Stir to combine.
6. Add the dressing, and toss.

✳ **VARIATION TIP:** If you love fresh herbs, add ¾ cup fresh parsley to this salad. Scallions or sliced red onion are also great additions if you like a more intense flavor.

Per Serving: Calories: 311; Total fat: 14g; Saturated fat: 2g; Protein: 9g; Carbs: 39g; Sugar: 1g; Fiber: 5g; Sodium: 281mg

CILANTRO-LIME QUINOA SALAD WITH SWEET POTATO

SERVES: 4   **PREP TIME:** 10 minutes   **COOK TIME:** 35 minutes

This nutritious quinoa and sweet potato salad is a fantastic option for meal prep or make-ahead meals. Often classified as a whole grain, quinoa is technically a seed and a great gluten-free alternative. I use white quinoa here, but black and red quinoa (or a combination) work equally well.

- 1 medium sweet potato, cut into ½-inch chunks
- 1 shallot, coarsely chopped
- 1 tablespoon extra-virgin olive oil
- Kosher salt
- Freshly ground black pepper
- 1 cup quinoa, rinsed
- 2 cups water
- Grated zest and juice of 1 lime
- 2 tablespoons finely chopped fresh cilantro

---

1. Preheat the oven to 400°F.
2. Spread the sweet potato and shallot out in an 8-by-8-inch glass baking dish. Drizzle with the oil. Season with salt and pepper.
3. Transfer the baking dish to the oven, and bake for 20 minutes. Stir well, and bake for 10 to 15 minutes more, or until the sweet potato is fork tender. Remove from the oven.
4. Meanwhile, in a medium saucepan, combine the quinoa and water. Bring to a boil over high heat.
5. Reduce the heat to low. Cover, and simmer for 15 minutes, or until the water has been absorbed. Remove from the heat. Let sit covered for 5 minutes.
6. In a large serving bowl, stir together the quinoa, sweet potato, and shallot.
7. Add the lime zest, lime juice, and cilantro. Stir well. Taste, and season with salt and pepper. Serve.

PREP TIP: When cooking quinoa, I highly recommend first giving it a good rinse in a fine-mesh sieve to remove its natural coating, which lends a bitter taste.

Per Serving: Calories: 219; Total fat: 6g; Saturated fat: 1g; Protein: 7g; Carbs: 35g; Sugar: 2g; Fiber: 4g; Sodium: 60mg

ROASTED BROCCOLI AND CARROT QUINOA WITH BROWNED BUTTER

SERVES: 4 **PREP TIME:** 10 minutes **COOK TIME:** 25 minutes

Brown butter is made by cooking butter until melted and the milk solids start to turn into brown specks, creating an amazing sauce with a slightly nutty aroma. Brown butter sauce is typically used in dishes like ravioli and seared scallops, but it packs a punch of flavor for the quinoa, broccoli, and carrot in this dish.

1 cup quinoa, thoroughly rinsed	**1 cup finely diced carrot**	**Freshly ground black pepper**
2 cups water	**1 tablespoon extra-virgin olive oil**	**3 tablespoons unsalted butter**
4 cups fresh broccoli florets	**Kosher salt**	**2 tablespoons fresh basil leaves, thinly sliced**

1. Preheat the oven to 400°F.

2. In a medium saucepan, combine the quinoa and water. Bring to a boil over high heat.

3. Reduce the heat to low. Cover, and simmer for 15 minutes, or until the water has been absorbed. Remove from the heat. Let sit covered for 5 minutes.

4. While the quinoa simmers, arrange the broccoli and carrot on a large sheet pan. Drizzle with the oil. Season with salt and pepper.

5. Transfer the sheet pan to the oven, and roast, stirring once or twice, for 15 to 20 minutes, or until the broccoli is browned in spots. Remove from the oven.

6. In a large mixing bowl, combine the cooked quinoa and the broccoli mixture. Stir well.

7. In a small skillet, melt the butter over medium heat. Continue cooking, stirring often, for 2 to 3 minutes, or until it turns into a rich, golden brown color. Then immediately remove from the heat, and pour over the quinoa mixture.

8. Add the basil, and stir well. Taste, and season with salt and pepper. Serve.

✳ VARIATION TIP: If you don't need the dish to be gluten-free, you can substitute couscous, prepared according to the package directions, for the quinoa.

Per Serving: Calories: 307; Total fat: 15g; Saturated fat: 6g; Protein: 9g; Carbs: 36g; Sugar: 3g; Fiber: 6g; Sodium: 94mg

EARTHY LENTIL AND RICE PILAF (DF) (GF) (NF) (OP) (VG)

SERVES: 6   **PREP TIME:** 5 minutes   **COOK TIME:** 50 to 55 minutes

The trick for making the best lentils and rice in one pot is to avoid stirring the pot too much after the rice goes in. Stirring will release the starches into the cooking liquid and make the whole mixture sticky and less appetizing. Find a nice low simmer, cover the pot, and let it rest before fluffing with a fork.

¼ cup extra-virgin olive oil
1 large onion, chopped
6 cups water

1 teaspoon ground cumin
1 teaspoon kosher salt

2 cups dried brown lentils,
   picked over and rinsed
1 cup basmati rice

---

1. In a medium pot, combine the oil and onion. Cook over medium heat for 7 to 10 minutes, or until the edges have browned.

2. Increase the heat to high. Add the water, cumin, and salt. Bring to a boil. Cook for about 3 minutes.

3. Add the lentils. Reduce the heat to medium-low. Cover the pot, and cook, stirring occasionally, for 20 minutes.

4. Stir in the rice, and cover. Cook for 20 minutes. Remove from the heat. Using a fork, fluff the rice. Serve warm.

SUBSTITUTION TIP: Use chicken or vegetable broth in place of the water to give the dish a flavor boost.

Per Serving: Calories: 433; Total fat: 10g; Saturated fat: 1g; Protein: 18g; Carbs: 68g; Sugar: 2g; Fiber: 8g; Sodium: 394mg

BULGUR AND CHICKPEA PILAF

SERVES: 6   **PREP TIME:** 5 minutes   **COOK TIME:** 25 minutes

A whole-wheat grain that is popular in Middle Eastern cuisine, bulgur is a versatile ingredient and hearty accompaniment to the chickpeas in this dish. It also pairs well with other proteins like fish, lamb, or chicken. Coarse bulgur wheat holds its shape and works best in a recipe like this, but if only medium coarse or fine bulgur is available, feel free to use it, and decrease the cooking time accordingly.

3 tablespoons extra-virgin olive oil

1 large onion, chopped

1 (16-ounce) can chickpeas, drained and rinsed

2 cups coarse bulgur wheat, rinsed and drained

1½ teaspoons kosher salt

½ teaspoon ground cinnamon

4 cups water

1. In a large pot, combine the oil and onion. Cook over medium heat for 5 minutes.

2. Add the chickpeas, and cook for 5 minutes.

3. Add the bulgur, salt, cinnamon, and water. Stir to combine.

4. Reduce the heat to low. Cover the pot, and cook for 10 minutes. Remove from the heat. Using a fork, fluff the pilaf. Cover, and let sit for 5 minutes.

VARIATION TIP: Garnish this dish with fresh chopped parsley, or pair it with a salad, tzatziki, or plain Greek yogurt.

Per Serving: Calories: 347; Total fat: 9g; Saturated fat: 1g; Protein: 12g; Carbs: 59g; Sugar: 3g; Fiber: 12g; Sodium: 587mg

ROASTED
CAULIFLOWER STEAKS
WITH HARISSA

P. 96

6

VEGETABLE MAINS

LENTIL QUESADILLAS

SERVES: 4   **PREP TIME:** 10 minutes   **COOK TIME:** 15 minutes

You'll want to make your own dang quesadilla with this dynamite recipe. When you're short on time, the combination of lentils, tortillas, and cheese will provide a fast but nutritious meal. The quesadillas are baked in the oven so you can make them all at once. And if you want to eat them with a side of tots, I won't blame you.

4 (6-inch) whole-wheat tortillas, divided

1 tablespoon extra-virgin olive oil, divided

1 (15-ounce) can lentils, drained and rinsed

1 yellow bell pepper, cored and finely chopped

1 tomato, diced

½ cup feta cheese, crumbled

1. Preheat the oven to 450°F. Line a sheet pan with parchment paper.
2. Place 2 tortillas on the prepared sheet pan, and brush with ½ tablespoon of oil. Flip the tortillas over so the oiled side is on the bottom.
3. Evenly divide the lentils between the tortillas, and spread them out.
4. Evenly divide the bell pepper, tomato, and cheese between the tortillas.
5. Top with the remaining 2 tortillas, and brush the tops with the remaining ½ tablespoon of oil.
6. Transfer the sheet pan to the oven, and bake, flipping once, for about 15 minutes, or until the tortillas are crispy and lightly browned. Remove from the oven.
7. Cut the quesadillas into quarters, and serve.

COOKING TIP: Try making quesadillas on the grill, cooking them over low heat for about 3 minutes per side, instead of cooking them in the oven. It gives them a spectacular smoky flavor.

Per Serving: Calories: 311; Total fat: 12g; Saturated fat: 5g; Protein: 14g; Carbs: 39g; Sugar: 4g; Fiber: 11g; Sodium: 386mg

VEGETABLE MEATBALLS AND CAULIFLOWER KORMA

SERVES: 4 **PREP TIME:** 10 minutes **COOK TIME:** 30 minutes

Inspired by Indian cuisine, this curry dish uses pantry and freezer ingredients, making it an ideal last-minute meal. Korma is typically a rich yogurt- or cream-based sauce with a variety of aromatics, spices, and cashews. If you find that your store-bought korma sauce could use a little more flavor, try amping up the flavor by adding a dash or two of garam masala. Serve this over a bowl of basmati rice or with garlic naan.

2 tablespoons vegetable oil

1 large yellow onion, chopped

4 garlic cloves, minced

2 (12-ounce) packages frozen vegetable meatballs

1 (12-ounce) package frozen cauliflower

1 (15-ounce) jar korma curry sauce

1 cup water

Kosher salt

1. In a large nonstick saucepan, heat the oil over medium heat.
2. Add the onion, and cook, stirring occasionally, for 5 to 6 minutes, or until the onion has softened.
3. Add the garlic, and cook for 1 minute.
4. Add the meatballs, cauliflower, korma sauce, and water. Season with salt.
5. Stir, cover, and simmer for 15 to 20 minutes, or until meatballs and cauliflower are fully cooked. Taste, and season with salt. Remove from the heat.

VARIATION TIP: For brighter flavors, you can stir in 1 to 2 tablespoons lemon juice and add 2 tablespoons chopped cilantro after the stew has fully cooked.

Per Serving: Calories: 527; Total fat: 29g; Saturated fat: 7g; Protein: 40g; Carbs: 27g; Sugar: 8g; Fiber: 12g; Sodium: 960mg

ROASTED CAULIFLOWER STEAKS WITH HARISSA

(DF) (GF) (NF) (V)

SERVES: 4 **PREP TIME:** 15 minutes **COOK TIME:** 50 minutes

The key ingredient to this cauliflower dish is harissa paste, which is a North African condiment made with simple ingredients, like dried chiles, garlic, oil, vinegar, and spices. It can usually be found in the spice aisle of any supermarket, but if it's not available, sriracha or red pepper flakes will work in a pinch.

---

2 heads cauliflower, outer leaves removed and stems trimmed

⅓ cup extra-virgin olive oil

1 teaspoon kosher salt

½ cup harissa paste

2 tablespoons honey

2 tablespoons freshly squeezed lemon juice

¼ teaspoon freshly ground black pepper

1 tablespoon toasted white sesame seeds

---

1. Preheat the oven to 425°F. Line a sheet pan with aluminum foil.

2. Put 1 head of cauliflower on a cutting board. Using a large, sharp knife, cut in half lengthwise through the center. Then cut each half into 1-inch-thick steaks. Repeat the process with the second head of cauliflower.

3. Arrange the cauliflower steaks in a single layer on the prepared sheet pan.

4. In a small bowl, whisk together the oil, salt, and harissa paste.

5. Spread the mixture over both sides of each cauliflower steak.

6. Transfer the sheet pan to the oven, and bake, turning once halfway through, for 40 to 50 minutes, or until the cauliflower is tender. Remove from the oven. Transfer to a serving platter.

7. To make the sauce, in a separate small bowl, whisk together the honey, lemon juice, and pepper until combined.

8. Drizzle the sauce over the steaks, and sprinkle with the sesame seeds before serving.

✳ **VARIATION TIP:** If desired, garnish the dish with 2 tablespoons chopped cilantro or parsley.

Per Serving: Calories: 280; Total fat: 20g; Saturated fat: 3g; Protein: 6g; Carbs: 25g; Sugar: 15g; Fiber: 7g; Sodium: 882mg

SWEET POTATO AND BLACK BEAN CRISPY TACOS

SERVES: 4   **PREP TIME**: 5 minutes   **COOK TIME**: 15 minutes

It doesn't have to be a Tuesday for me to want tacos. In fact, I could eat tacos every day of the week and be satisfied. These tacos are a great choice whenever I want a meatless, lighter version. They're easy to make and even easier to serve because everyone assembles their own at the table.

1 (10-ounce) package frozen
   roasted sweet potatoes
Kosher salt
Freshly ground black pepper
4 (8-inch) flour tortillas

1 to 2 tablespoons extra-virgin
   olive oil
1 cup canned vegetarian
   refried black beans
½ cup guacamole

1 cup queso fresco or
   feta cheese, crumbled,
   for topping

1. Cook the sweet potatoes according to the package directions. Discard any excess water. Season with salt and pepper.

2. Heat a large nonstick skillet over medium heat. Lightly brush both sides of each tortilla with the oil.

3. Working in batches, put the tortillas in the skillet, and cook for 1 to 2 minutes per side, or until lightly brown and crispy. Remove from the heat. Transfer to a flat surface.

4. Spread the beans in the center of each tortilla, then top each with a quarter of the sweet potatoes, guacamole, and cheese.

SUBSTITUTION TIP: If you are not familiar with queso fresco, or "fresh cheese," it's a crumbly and mild Mexican cheese available at most supermarkets alongside other Mexican cheeses. Feta cheese makes for a suitable substitute.

VARIATION TIP: You may replace flour tortillas with gluten-free, whole-wheat, or spinach tortillas according to your preference and needs—or even use crunchy taco shells. But avoid using corn tortillas because they can break apart easily. Chopped cilantro and sour cream can be added as toppings if you have either of them on hand.

Per Serving: Calories: 436; Total fat: 19g; Saturated fat: 7g; Protein: 15g; Carbs: 53g; Sugar: 6g; Fiber: 9g; Sodium: 713mg

SWEET POTATO AND
BLACK BEAN
CRISPY TACOS

P. 97

GRILLED EGGPLANT ROLLS

MAKES: 4 rolls   **PREP TIME:** 30 minutes   **COOK TIME:** 10 minutes, plus 5 minutes to cool

Filled with creamy ricotta and goat cheese, this eggplant recipe is something that vegetarians and meat-eaters alike will enjoy. It can be served as a great meatless main or a tasty side dish to your favorite entrée. Try them with Lemon Orzo with Fresh Herbs (page 73) or Swordfish in Red Sauce (page 145).

---

2 large eggplants
1 teaspoon kosher salt
4 ounces goat cheese
1 cup ricotta cheese

¼ cup fresh basil leaves,
 finely chopped
½ teaspoon freshly ground
 black pepper

Olive oil cooking spray,
 for coating

---

1. Trim off the tops of the eggplants, and cut the eggplants lengthwise into ¼-inch-thick slices. Sprinkle the slices with the salt, and put the eggplant in a colander for 15 to 20 minutes. The salt will draw out excess water from the eggplant.

2. In a large bowl, combine the goat cheese, ricotta cheese, basil, and pepper.

3. Preheat a grill, grill pan, or skillet on medium heat. (If using a skillet, lightly oil with cooking spray.)

4. Using a paper towel, pat the eggplant slices dry. Lightly spray with cooking spray.

5. Put the eggplant on the grill, and cook for 3 minutes per side. Remove from the heat. Let cool for 5 minutes.

6. To roll, lay 1 eggplant slice flat, place 1 tablespoon of the cheese mixture at the base of the slice, and roll up. Repeat with the remaining eggplant slices and cheese mixture. Serve immediately, or chill until ready to serve.

✱ VARIATION TIP: This recipe can also be made using grilled zucchini. For a punch of citrus flavor, try adding 1 teaspoon lemon zest to the filling.

Per Serving: Calories: 252; Total fat: 14g; Saturated fat: 9g; Protein: 15g; Carbs: 18g; Sugar: 10g; Fiber: 8g; Sodium: 769mg

TOMATO, POTATO, AND EGG SALAD   (DF) (GF) (NF) (V)

SERVES: 4   **PREP TIME:** 10 minutes   **COOK TIME:** 25 minutes, plus time to cool

My family isn't the biggest fan of mayonnaise so I'm always looking for ways to change up the classic potato salad. You won't even miss the mayonnaise in this oil-based potato and egg salad recipe. With the addition of fresh herbs and tomatoes, it tastes a little lighter and allows the other ingredients to really shine.

---

2 pounds medium russet
  potatoes
6 large eggs
3 medium vine-ripened
  tomatoes, cut into
  1-inch pieces

¼ cup extra-virgin olive oil,
  plus more as needed
Kosher salt

1 teaspoon dried oregano
2 tablespoons chopped fresh
  basil leaves

---

1. Fill a large stockpot halfway with cold water. Add the potatoes and eggs. Bring to a boil over high heat. Cook for about 20 minutes, or until the potatoes are fork tender. Remove from the heat. Using a slotted spoon, remove the potatoes and eggs, and set aside. Let cool before handling.

2. In a large salad bowl, combine the tomatoes and oil. Season with salt. Toss to coat.

3. Peel the potatoes, and cut into 1-inch dice.

4. Peel the eggs, quarter, then cut again into 3 or 4 smaller pieces.

5. Add the potatoes and eggs to the tomatoes. Mix well.

6. Stir in the oregano and basil. Add more oil as needed. Serve immediately while still warm.

✳ VARIATION TIP: Instead of using russet potatoes, you can use red or white baby potatoes. Because there is no need to peel them, it's quicker, too.

Per Serving: Calories: 423; Total fat: 21g; Saturated fat: 4g; Protein: 15g; Carbs: 45g; Sugar: 4g; Fiber: 4g; Sodium: 162mg

TOSSED LENTIL SALAD WITH FETA CHEESE

SERVES: 4   **PREP TIME:** 10 minutes   **COOK TIME:** 30 to 35 minutes

Fresh or dried herbs can add an earthy flavor to any salad dressing. For this tossed salad, I sometimes like to add a pinch of dried oregano to the dressing and garnish with freshly chopped basil. This salad is great for meal prep, because the lentils and vinaigrette can be made ahead. For quick lunches and dinners during the week, toss all the salad ingredients together right before serving.

---

3 cups water
1 cup dried brown or green lentils, picked over and rinsed

1½ teaspoons kosher salt, divided
2 large ripe tomatoes, diced
2 Persian cucumbers, diced

⅓ cup freshly squeezed lemon juice
½ cup extra-virgin olive oil
1 cup crumbled feta cheese

---

1. In a large pot, combine the water, lentils, and 1 teaspoon of salt. Bring to a simmer over medium heat.

2. Reduce the heat to low. Cover the pot, and cook, stirring occasionally, for 30 minutes, or until the lentils no longer have a crunch but still hold their form. You should be able to smoosh the lentil between your two fingers when pinched. Remove from the heat. Drain in a colander, and transfer to a large bowl.

3. Add the tomatoes and cucumbers.

4. To make the dressing, in a small bowl, whisk together the lemon juice, oil, and remaining ½ teaspoon of salt.

5. Pour the dressing over the lentils and vegetables.

6. Add the cheese, and gently toss.

✻ **COOKING TIP:** For this recipe, you want the lentils to keep their shape when cooked. Because lentils tend to become mushy when overcooked, I like to check for doneness 5 minutes before the timer is up.

Per Serving: Calories: 540; Total fat: 36g; Saturated fat: 9g; Protein: 19g; Carbs: 39g; Sugar: 7g; Fiber: 7g; Sodium: 645mg

TWICE-BAKED SWEET POTATOES WITH ONION, GARLIC, AND SPINACH

SERVES: 4 **PREP TIME:** 10 minutes **COOK TIME:** 1 hour 15 minutes

Baked, mashed, roasted, or fried, a sweet potato can be the star of any meal. Though sweet potatoes are tasty on their own, stuffing them with other wholesome ingredients like onion, garlic, and spinach takes them to a new level.

---

4 large sweet potatoes

1 tablespoon extra-virgin olive oil

1 medium yellow onion, diced

Kosher salt

Freshly ground black pepper

2 cups baby spinach, chopped

4 garlic cloves, minced

---

1. Preheat the oven to 400°F.

2. Using a fork, prick the sweet potatoes along the tops 3 or 4 times.

3. Place the sweet potatoes in the oven on the top rack with a sheet pan on a rack below. Bake for 40 to 50 minutes, or until fork tender. Remove from the oven. Let cool.

4. Halve the sweet potatoes lengthwise. Scoop the insides into a medium mixing bowl, and mash thoroughly. Set aside the scooped-out skins.

5. In a large skillet, heat the oil over medium heat.

6. Add the onion. Season with salt and pepper. Cook, stirring occasionally, for about 8 minutes, or until beginning to brown. Remove from the heat. Transfer to the bowl with the mashed sweet potatoes.

7. Add the spinach and garlic. Stir well to combine. Season with salt and pepper.

8. Scoop the sweet potato mixture back into the skins.

9. Put the sweet potatoes on a sheet pan.

10. Transfer the sheet pan to the oven, and bake for 10 to 15 minutes, or until the sweet potatoes are hot. Remove from the oven. Serve.

PREP TIP: You can bake the sweet potatoes the first time and store them in the refrigerator uncut up to 2 days in advance.

Per Serving: Calories: 161; Total fat: 4g; Saturated fat: 1g; Protein: 3g; Carbs: 30g; Sugar: 7g; Fiber: 5g; Sodium: 124mg

SPAGHETTI SQUASH POMODORO

SERVES: 4   **PREP TIME:** 10 minutes   **COOK TIME:** 30 minutes

Spaghetti squash has become a popular gluten-free alternative to pasta for good reason. I love to make this healthy swap whenever a pasta craving hits. Instead of roasting the spaghetti squash in the oven, you can take a shortcut by cooking it in the microwave on high for about 15 minutes, turning the squash halfway through cooking.

1 spaghetti squash

Nonstick cooking spray, for coating the squash

2 cups diced fresh tomatoes

1 garlic clove, minced

1 tablespoon finely chopped fresh basil leaves

Kosher salt

Freshly ground black pepper

1. Preheat the oven to 375°F.

2. Halve the spaghetti squash lengthwise. Scoop out and discard the seeds and stringy insides. Spray with cooking spray.

3. Place each squash half, cut-side down, on a sheet pan.

4. Transfer the sheet pan to the oven, and bake for 30 minutes, or until the squash can easily be pricked with a fork. Remove from the oven. Scrape a fork across the inside cavity to shred the squash into spaghetti-like threads. Continue until you reach the shell.

5. In a medium mixing bowl, stir together the tomatoes, garlic, and basil. Season with salt and pepper.

6. To serve, divide the spaghetti squash evenly among 4 plates. Top each one with a quarter of the tomato mixture, and serve.

✳ **VARIATION TIP:** After shredding the spaghetti squash, put it back inside the shell, and top each half with half of the tomato mixture. Serve in the shell on serving dishes.

✳ **SUBSTITUTION TIP:** You can substitute canned diced tomatoes for the fresh tomatoes. Drain before adding them in step 5.

Per Serving: Calories: 81; Total fat: 1g; Saturated fat: 0g; Protein: 2g; Carbs: 18g; Sugar: 8g; Fiber: 4g; Sodium: 78mg

QUICK THAI-STYLE RED CURRY WITH VEGETABLES

(30) (DF) (GF) (NF) (OP) (VG)

SERVES: 4 **PREP TIME:** 5 minutes **COOK TIME:** 25 minutes

Add some kick to your meatless meals with this delicious and veggie-packed Thai-style red curry. The ingredients are found in most grocery stores, and it's a breeze to make. Although the stir-fry vegetable blend I use contains broccoli, cauliflower, carrots, and red bell pepper, this recipe is versatile enough to accept other combinations of vegetables, such as mushrooms, kale, and butternut squash.

1 (13½-ounce) can coconut milk

2 tablespoons Thai red curry paste

1 tablespoon light brown sugar

Kosher salt

Freshly ground black pepper

2 (16-ounce) bags frozen stir-fry vegetables

1 tablespoon finely chopped fresh cilantro

1. In a large sauté pan, combine the coconut milk, curry paste, and sugar. Heat over medium heat, stirring until combined. Taste, and season with salt and pepper. Bring to a boil.

2. Reduce the heat to medium-low. Simmer for 5 minutes.

3. Stir in the frozen stir-fry vegetables.

4. Cover the pan, and increase the heat to medium. Cook for 10 to 15 minutes, or until the vegetables have thawed. Remove from the heat.

5. Stir in the cilantro. Taste, and adjust the seasonings. Serve.

✳ **SUBSTITUTION TIP:** You can substitute 4 cups fresh vegetables for frozen ones. Note that some vegetables may need additional cooking time, may need to be precooked before adding, or both.

Per Serving: Calories: 371; Total fat: 22g; Saturated fat: 18g; Protein: 10g; Carbs: 37g; Sugar: 2g; Fiber: 11g; Sodium: 160mg

MISO-BLACK BEAN BURGER PATTIES

SERVES: 4   **PREP TIME:** 10 minutes   **COOK TIME:** 25 minutes

Miso is a fermented paste made from soybeans, commonly used as a seasoning in Japanese cuisine. It is earthy and salty and gives sauces, soups, and marinades a depth of flavor. In this recipe, the black bean patties boast plenty of umami thanks to the addition of miso. Serve these patties with lettuce wraps for a lighter, bun-free burger.

1 (15-ounce) can black beans, drained and rinsed

2 teaspoons miso

½ teaspoon onion powder

½ teaspoon garlic powder

¼ cup fine dried bread crumbs

¼ teaspoon kosher salt

¼ teaspoon freshly ground black pepper

2 tablespoons water

1. Preheat the oven to 350°F. Line a sheet pan with parchment paper.
2. Using paper towels, pat the beans dry. Put the beans, miso, onion powder, garlic powder, bread crumbs, salt, pepper, and water in a food processor. Pulse until the mixture comes together and is sticky.
3. Divide the black bean mixture into 4 even portions, and form into patties.
4. Arrange the patties in a single layer on the prepared sheet pan.
5. Transfer the sheet pan to the oven, and bake, flipping about halfway through, for 22 minutes, or until the patties are lightly golden on both sides. Remove from the oven. Serve, or let cool. If you are serving them later, reheat in a hot pan with a bit of oil.

✳ PREP TIP: If you don't have a food processor, you can mash all the ingredients together using a potato masher.

Per Serving: Calories: 107; Total fat: 1g; Saturated fat: 0g; Protein: 7g; Carbs: 19g; Sugar: 0g; Fiber: 6g; Sodium: 278mg

MEATLESS MEATLOAF

(GF) (NF) (V)

SERVES: 6   **PREP TIME:** 15 minutes, plus 10 minutes to rest   **COOK TIME:** 1 hour 35 minutes

This meatless "meatloaf" is hearty, filling, and fantastic for meal prep. Want to make it a day in advance? Go ahead and prep the mixture, then just cover it and put it in the refrigerator. The day you are serving the loaf, bake as directed. The meatloaf will take a bit more time to cook because it is in a chilled pan.

---

1 cup dried lentils, rinsed

3 cups water

2 teaspoons extra-virgin
 olive oil

½ cup minced onion

2 cups chopped mushrooms

2 tablespoons minced garlic

1 teaspoon kosher salt

¼ teaspoon freshly ground
 black pepper

½ cup plain Greek yogurt

---

1. Preheat the oven to 350°F.

2. In a medium pot, combine the lentils and water. Bring to a boil over high heat.

3. Reduce the heat to low. Simmer for 25 to 30 minutes, or until the lentils are tender. Remove from the heat. Let sit for 10 minutes. Drain in a sieve. Transfer to a food processor, and puree. (Or mash in a bowl with a potato masher.)

4. Add the oil and onion to a medium skillet, and cook for 5 minutes over medium heat.

5. Reduce the heat to medium-low. Add the mushroom, garlic, salt, and pepper, and cook for 8 to 10 minutes, or until all the moisture has been cooked out of the mushrooms. Remove from the heat. Transfer to the food processor with the lentils.

6. Add the yogurt, and puree.

7. Put the mixture into an 8½-by-4½-inch loaf pan, and pat down to pack it in tightly. Cover with aluminum foil.

8. Transfer the loaf pan to the oven, and bake for 45 minutes. Remove from the oven. Leave the loaf in the pan, and let cool for 10 minutes before slicing and serving.

✳ **PREP TIP:** Use brown lentils for best results because they are tender when cooked and give the best texture to the meatloaf. But if you have another variety of lentils on hand, go ahead and use them.

Per Serving: Calories: 153; Total fat: 3g; Saturated fat: 1g; Protein: 10g; Carbs: 24g; Sugar: 3g; Fiber: 4g; Sodium: 401mg

ROASTED EGGPLANT PITAS

SERVES: 4 **PREP TIME:** 10 minutes **COOK TIME:** 10 minutes

Pita bread is naturally hollow, and the space inside is excellent for filling with savory ingredients. This sandwich is packed with roasted eggplant, which has a nice meaty texture. Boost the protein content by spreading some hummus or Smoky Eggplant Dip (page 30) on the inside of the pita bread.

---

2 medium purple
   eggplants, sliced
2 tablespoons extra-virgin
   olive oil
Kosher salt

Freshly ground black pepper
¼ cup plain Greek yogurt
Juice of ½ lemon
3 whole-wheat pita
   rounds, halved

1 small red onion, thinly sliced
Fresh mint leaves, for garnish
   (optional)

---

1. Place an oven rack 4 to 6 inches from the broiler. Preheat the oven to 400°F. Line a roasting pan with aluminum foil.

2. Put the eggplant slices in the prepared pan. Brush both sides with the oil. Season with salt and pepper.

3. Transfer the pan to the oven, and broil for 4 minutes per side, or until the eggplant looks collapsed and puckered. Remove from the oven.

4. In a small bowl, combine the yogurt and lemon juice. Season with salt and pepper.

5. Fill each pita half evenly with the yogurt mixture, eggplant, onion, and mint leaves (if using). Serve.

✳ **VARIATION TIP:** For extra crunch, I like adding finely chopped iceberg lettuce to each pita.

Per Serving: Calories: 274; Total fat: 9g; Saturated fat: 2g; Protein: 8g; Carbs: 45g; Sugar: 12g; Fiber: 12g; Sodium: 265mg

VEGETABLE QUESADILLAS

SERVES: 3   **PREP TIME:** 5 minutes   **COOK TIME:** 25 minutes

Whenever people ask me for easy dinner ideas, I'm always quick to recommend quesadillas. This crowd-pleasing favorite also makes for a great game-day appetizer for your vegetarian fans. Try a mix of melty cheeses to experiment with flavor profiles. Serve guacamole and salsa alongside the quesadillas for an even more filling meal.

---

1 tablespoon extra-virgin olive oil

1 cup chopped bell peppers, any colors

½ cup thinly sliced mushrooms

¼ cup thinly sliced red onion

6 (9-inch) flour tortillas

1½ cups shredded Mexican cheese blend, divided

---

1. In a skillet, heat the oil over medium-high heat.

2. Add the bell peppers, mushrooms, and onion. Cook for about 5 minutes, or until just tender. Transfer to a bowl.

3. Put 1 tortilla in the skillet, sprinkle about ¼ cup of cheese over the tortilla, and top with a third of the vegetable mixture. Sprinkle with another ¼ cup of cheese, then top with 1 more tortilla. Cook for about 2 to 3 minutes per side, or until golden on both sides. Transfer to a cutting board. Using a pizza cutter, cut into triangles. Repeat the process 2 more times with the remaining tortillas, cheese, and vegetables. Serve.

VARIATION TIP: For a different flavor, you can replace ½ cup chopped bell peppers with ½ cup chopped zucchini—or whatever other vegetable you like that's in season.

Per Serving: Calories: 549; Total fat: 26g; Saturated fat: 11g; Protein: 22g; Carbs: 55g; Sugar: 7g; Fiber: 4g; Sodium: 767mg

ROASTED CHICKEN
WITH THAI-INSPIRED
MANGO SALAD

P. 112

7

POULTRY

ROASTED CHICKEN WITH THAI-INSPIRED MANGO SALAD

(30) (DF) (GF) (NF)

SERVES: 4   **PREP TIME:** 10 minutes   **COOK TIME:** 20 minutes

This fresh and vibrant Thai-inspired mango salad is one delicious, nutrient-rich, and filling recipe. Served warm or chilled, chicken breast is mixed with juicy slices of mango and crisp butter lettuce, all coated in a zingy lime and chili dressing. For faster prep, use a store-bought rotisserie chicken.

Nonstick cooking spray, for coating the roasting pan

4 boneless, skinless chicken breasts

3 tablespoons extra-virgin olive oil, divided

Kosher salt

Freshly ground black pepper

1½ tablespoons sriracha

¼ cup freshly squeezed lime juice

1 pound unripe mango, peeled, pitted, and thinly sliced

8 butter lettuce leaves, coarsely chopped

1. Preheat the oven to 425°F. Coat a roasting pan with cooking spray.

2. Coat the chicken with 1 tablespoon of oil. Season with salt and pepper.

3. Arrange the chicken in a single layer in the prepared roasting pan.

4. Transfer the roasting pan to the oven, and roast for 15 to 20 minutes, or until the chicken is cooked through but still moist. Remove from the oven. Let cool slightly, then slice.

5. In a large bowl, whisk together the sriracha, lime juice, and remaining 2 tablespoons of oil. Season with salt and pepper.

6. Add the mango, lettuce, and chicken. Toss to combine, and serve.

✳ PREP TIP: Unripe mangos are firmer and not nearly as sweet as the ripe ones. To pick one, press the mango gently, and choose one that feels very firm.

✳ VARIATION TIP: You can add a bit more flavor and texture to this salad by sprinkling it with 1 cup chopped fresh cilantro and 2 tablespoons chopped peanuts.

Per Serving: Calories: 295; Total fat: 13g; Saturated fat: 2g; Protein: 28g; Carbs: 19g; Sugar: 16g; Fiber: 2g; Sodium: 155mg

PAN CHICKEN WITH TOMATOES

SERVES: 4   **PREP TIME:** 5 minutes   **COOK TIME:** 15 minutes

Winner, winner, chicken dinner! This hearty one-pot dish has lots of bold flavors—pungent garlic, sweet cherry tomatoes, and briny olives combined with sautéed chicken. It's a delightful meal you'll want to add to your dinner rotation. Serve it with Angel Hair Pasta with Garlic Spinach (page 77) or Earthy Lentil and Rice Pilaf (page 89).

3 tablespoons extra-virgin olive oil

2 garlic cloves, minced

1 pint cherry tomatoes, halved

1 teaspoon kosher salt

1 pound chicken tenders, cut into 4 or 5 pieces

1 teaspoon dried oregano

¼ cup black or green olives, pitted

1. In a large sauté pan, combine the oil and garlic. Cook over low heat for 1 minute.

2. Increase the heat to medium. Add the tomatoes and salt. Cook for about 5 minutes, or until the tomatoes burst and cook down.

3. Add the chicken and oregano. Mix well.

4. Add the olives. Cook for about 10 minutes, or until the chicken is no longer pink. Remove from the heat.

SUBSTITUTION TIP: Fresh cherry tomatoes offer liveliness to this dish, but if you are looking to dress some pasta with the sauce and turn this recipe into a two-course meal, use 2 cups canned crushed tomatoes instead.

Per Serving: Calories: 236; Total fat: 13g; Saturated fat: 2g; Protein: 26g; Carbs: 3g; Sugar: 1g; Fiber: 1g; Sodium: 604mg

BRAISED CHICKEN AND MUSHROOMS

SERVES: 4   **PREP TIME:** 20 minutes   **COOK TIME:** 1 hour 30 minutes

The word "braise" may sound daunting, but it's really just a fancy way of saying "brown the meat, then simmer in some liquid." Not so daunting now, right? Boneless, skinless chicken thighs lend themselves well to this method of cooking, whereas chicken breasts tend to dry out. The mushrooms will add extra meatiness and a depth of flavor you'll really enjoy.

---

3 tablespoons extra-virgin olive oil

8 pieces chicken thighs and drumsticks

1½ cups garlic cloves, peeled

1 large onion, chopped

1 pound cremini mushrooms, cleaned and halved

1 teaspoon kosher salt

4 cups low-sodium chicken broth

---

1. In a large pot or Dutch oven, heat the oil over medium heat.

2. Add the chicken, and brown on all sides for about 8 minutes total. Transfer to a dish.

3. Add the garlic, onion, mushrooms, and salt to the Dutch oven. Cook, stirring, for 8 minutes.

4. Add the broth, and stir everything together.

5. Reduce the heat to medium-low. Add the chicken, cover, and simmer for 1 hour.

6. Uncover, and simmer for 10 minutes, or until the sauce has reduced. Remove from the heat. Serve.

VARIATION TIP: This is great served on top of rice or noodles. You can also finish off the recipe with fresh chopped parsley for color and flavor.

Per Serving: Calories: 658; Total fat: 40g; Saturated fat: 10g; Protein: 49g; Carbs: 26g; Sugar: 4g; Fiber: 2g; Sodium: 695mg

ROAST CHICKEN WITH PAN GRAVY

SERVES: 4 **PREP TIME:** 15 minutes **COOK TIME:** 1 hour 40 minutes, plus 10 minutes to rest

In this roast chicken recipe, the pan drippings are used to make a gravy. Using cornstarch instead of flour is a good way to ensure your gravy stays lump-free. To round out the meal, put root vegetables, such as carrots and parsnips, in the roasting pan, set the chicken on top before roasting, and you'll be rewarded with flavor-packed vegetables.

---

1 (3- to 3½-pound) whole chicken

½ teaspoon kosher salt

¼ teaspoon freshly ground black pepper

2 teaspoons hot smoked paprika

1 teaspoon onion powder

2 tablespoons extra-virgin olive oil

¼ cup freshly squeezed orange juice

2 teaspoons cornstarch

½ cup water

---

1. Adjust the oven rack to the lower-middle position. Preheat the oven to 375°F.

2. Place the chicken on a rack in a roasting pan.

3. In a small bowl, combine the salt, pepper, paprika, onion powder, oil, and orange juice.

4. Using a brush, generously apply the mixture to the bird.

5. Transfer the roasting pan to the oven, and cook, basting with pan juices every 30 minutes, for 1¼ to 1½ hours, or until a thermometer inserted into thickest part of thigh registers 175°F and the breast registers at least 165°F. Remove from the oven. Carefully lift the rack with the chicken out of the pan, and set aside. Tent lightly with aluminum foil. Let rest for 10 minutes.

6. While the chicken rests, place the roasting pan on the stove over medium heat, and skim the fat. Bring the juices to a boil.

7. In another small bowl, mix together the cornstarch and water.

8. Slowly pour the cornstarch mixture into the pan, whisking to avoid lumps. When the sauce has thickened to a gravy-like consistency, remove from the heat.

9. Carve the chicken, and serve with the gravy.

Per Serving: Calories: 523; Total fat: 38g; Saturated fat: 10g; Protein: 39g; Carbs: 4g; Sugar: 1g; Fiber: 1g; Sodium: 437mg

SMOTHERED CHICKEN BREASTS WITH CARAMELIZED ONIONS AND PROVOLONE

(GF) (NF)

SERVES: 4   **PREP TIME:** 10 minutes   **COOK TIME:** 35 minutes, plus 5 minutes to rest

This oven-baked chicken breast recipe proves that boneless, skinless chicken breasts can truly be juicy and flavorful. Caramelizing onions until they are sweet and deeply golden brown is worth the wait, because they amp up the flavor and add complexity to all kinds of savory dishes. Serve this dish with a veggie side, like the Braised Green Beans with Tomatoes (see page 174).

1½ pounds boneless chicken breasts

1 teaspoon dried basil

Kosher salt

Freshly ground black pepper

2 tablespoons extra-virgin olive oil

2 yellow onions, halved and thinly sliced

1 tablespoon balsamic vinegar

4 ounces sliced provolone cheese

1. Preheat the oven to 400°F.

2. Put the chicken on a sheet pan, and rub the basil, salt, and pepper all over.

3. Transfer the sheet pan to the oven, and bake for 20 to 25 minutes, or until the chicken has cooked through. Remove from the oven, leaving the oven on. Let sit for 5 minutes.

4. Meanwhile, in a large skillet, heat the oil over medium-low heat.

5. Add the onions. Season with salt and pepper. Cook, stirring occasionally, for 20 to 25 minutes, or until golden brown.

6. Drizzle with the vinegar, and stir well. Cook for 2 to 3 minutes, or until the vinegar has been absorbed. Remove from the heat.

7. Cut the chicken into ¼-inch slices. Arrange in an oven-safe serving dish (or baking dish). Top with the onions and then the cheese.

8. Transfer the serving dish to the oven, and bake for 2 to 3 minutes, or until the cheese has melted. Remove from the oven. Serve.

✳ VARIATION TIP: Serve the chicken on sandwich rolls, with onions and cheese piled on top.

Per Serving: Calories: 321; Total fat: 17g; Saturated fat: 6g; Protein: 33g; Carbs: 7g; Sugar: 3g; Fiber: 1g; Sodium: 342mg

MAPLE- AND MUSTARD-GLAZED CHICKEN BREASTS

SERVES: 4   **PREP TIME:** 5 minutes   **COOK TIME:** 35 minutes

These juicy chicken breasts are your answer to a delicious weeknight dinner. The chicken is cooked in a skillet in a sweet and tangy maple-mustard sauce, which is made using common pantry items. Serve the chicken with Earthy Lentil and Rice Pilaf (page 89) and Crispy Breaded Cauliflower (page 178).

---

4 (6- to 8-ounce) boneless, skinless chicken breasts

½ teaspoon kosher salt

¼ teaspoon freshly ground black pepper

2 tablespoons extra-virgin olive oil, divided

1 large sweet onion, diced

1 tablespoon whole-grain mustard

2 tablespoons maple syrup

---

1. Using paper towels, pat the chicken dry. Season both sides with the salt and pepper.

2. In a large heavy skillet, heat 1 tablespoon of oil over medium heat.

3. Add the onion, and cook for 5 minutes. Transfer to a plate.

4. Reduce the heat to medium-low. Add the remaining 1 tablespoon of oil to the skillet.

5. Place the chicken, smooth-side down, in the skillet, and cook, without turning, for 10 minutes, or until golden brown.

6. Turn the chicken, and return the onion to the skillet. Cook, stirring the onion occasionally to keep it from browning too quickly, for 10 minutes.

7. In a small bowl, stir together the mustard and maple syrup.

8. Drizzle the mixture on top of the chicken. Cook for 5 minutes, or until the chicken is glazed and an instant-read thermometer registers 165°F or the juices run clear when the thickest part of the breast is pierced with a knife. Remove from the heat.

9. Plate the chicken, and stir together any remaining sauce and the onions. Ladle over the chicken to serve.

PREP TIP: I prefer whole-grain mustard in this recipe, but Dijon mustard works well, too.

Per Serving: Calories: 297; Total fat: 10g; Saturated fat: 2g; Protein: 40g; Carbs: 10g; Sugar: 8g; Fiber: 1g; Sodium: 452mg

CRISPY BAKED PANKO AND DIJON CHICKEN TENDERS

SERVES: 4   **PREP TIME:** 15 minutes   **COOK TIME:** 30 minutes

It's time to leave those fried chicken nuggets in the freezer! This crispy and healthy baked chicken tenders recipe will be a hit with both kids and adults. The coating can also be used for fish to make baked fish fingers.

2 cups panko bread crumbs

Nonstick cooking spray,
for coating

½ cup mayonnaise

1 tablespoon Dijon mustard

1 teaspoon freshly squeezed
lemon juice

1 pound chicken tenders

½ teaspoon kosher salt

¼ teaspoon freshly ground
black pepper

1. Preheat the oven to 225°F.

2. Put the panko on a rimmed sheet pan, and spritz with cooking spray.

3. Transfer the sheet pan to the oven, and toast for 4 to 5 minutes, or until the panko is light golden brown. Remove from the oven, leaving the oven on. Transfer to a shallow dish.

4. Increase the oven temperature to 425°F. Line a rimmed sheet pan with aluminum foil, and place a wire rack inside the sheet pan. Lightly coat the rack with cooking spray.

5. In a shallow dish, whisk together the mayonnaise, mustard, and lemon juice.

6. Using paper towels, pat the chicken dry. Season with the salt and pepper.

7. One at a time, dip each chicken tender in the mayonnaise mixture. Roll the chicken tender in the toasted panko until coated completely on all sides.

8. Place the coated tenders on the wire rack at least 2 inches apart, and lightly coat the top of the chicken tenders with cooking spray.

9. Transfer the sheet pan to the oven, and bake for 20 to 25 minutes, or until the chicken is golden brown and cooked through. Remove from the oven. Let cool on the rack for 5 minutes before serving.

✱ **SUBSTITUTION TIP:** You can use regular bread crumbs, but there will be a slight variation in texture.

Per Serving: Calories: 356; Total fat: 16g; Saturated fat: 3g; Protein: 30g; Carbs: 20g; Sugar: 2g; Fiber: 1g; Sodium: 573mg

CHEESY CHICKEN ENCHILADAS

(NF)

SERVES: 4   **PREP TIME:** 20 minutes   **COOK TIME:** 1 hour

Enchiladas are one of our family's favorites, and I'm happy to make them often, especially in the winter, when we're tired of the usual soups and stews. To make the assembly of this casserole as easy as possible, use chicken breasts from a rotisserie chicken and your favorite prepared enchilada sauce. I prefer red enchilada sauce, but green will work just as well here.

Nonstick cooking spray, for coating	Kosher salt	2 cups shredded Cheddar-Jack cheese, divided
2 (6- to 8-ounce) boneless, skinless chicken breasts	Freshly ground black pepper	
	3 cups red enchilada sauce	
	2 garlic cloves, minced	8 (7- to 8-inch) corn tortillas

1. Preheat the oven to 425°F. Lightly coat the bottom of a 9-by-13-inch casserole dish with cooking spray.

2. Season both sides of the chicken breasts with the salt and pepper.

3. In a deep skillet, combine the enchilada sauce and garlic. Bring to a boil over medium-high heat.

4. Add the chicken breasts to the skillet, and nestle into the sauce.

5. Reduce the heat to low. Cover the skillet, and cook for 15 to 20 minutes, or until the chicken has cooked through. Remove from the heat. Using tongs, transfer the chicken to a large bowl. Let the chicken and sauce cool for 5 minutes.

6. Using 2 forks, shred the chicken (see cooking tip).

7. Add ¾ cup of enchilada sauce and 1 cup of cheese. Gently stir to mix.

8. Wrap the tortillas in a damp paper towel, and warm in the microwave on high for 20 to 30 seconds, or until soft and pliable.

9. Spoon a heaping ⅓ cup of the chicken mixture down the center of each tortilla. Wrap the tortillas around the filling.

10. Place the tortillas, seam-side down, in the prepared casserole dish. Spritz the enchiladas with cooking spray.

Continued

11. Transfer the casserole dish to the oven, and bake for 10 minutes. Remove from the oven, leaving the oven on.

12. Reduce the oven temperature to 400°F.

13. Pour the remaining 2¼ cups of enchilada sauce over the enchiladas, and sprinkle with the remaining 1 cup of cheese.

14. Cover the dish with aluminum foil. Return to the oven, and bake for 20 minutes.

15. Remove the foil, and bake the enchiladas for 5 minutes, or until the cheese is melted and bubbly. Remove from the oven.

COOKING TIP: To shred chicken using 2 forks, pierce the chicken with one fork, and hold it steady while slowly scraping the other fork, prongs facing backward, away from the other fork.

Per Serving: Calories: 508; Total fat: 25g; Saturated fat: 12g; Protein: 38g; Carbs: 33g; Sugar: 5g; Fiber: 5g; Sodium: 921mg

CHICKEN EGG ROLL IN A BOWL

SERVES: 4   **PREP TIME:** 5 minutes   **COOK TIME:** 15 minutes

This egg roll in a bowl recipe has all the flavors of a traditional egg roll, cooked in a Dutch oven, without the fried wrapper! Not only is this great as leftovers, but I often double the recipe so I can have extra for lunch. If you crave a little crunch, top the bowls with some fried wonton strips or chow mein noodles.

1 tablespoon extra-virgin olive oil

1 pound ground chicken

1 (16-ounce) bag fresh coleslaw mix

⅓ cup Chinese-style stir-fry sauce, plus more for serving

2 scallions, both white and green parts, chopped

2 tablespoons sesame seeds

1. In a Dutch oven, heat the oil over medium-high heat.
2. Add the chicken, and brown, using a wooden spoon to break up the chunks, for 10 minutes, or until no longer pink.
3. Add the coleslaw mix, and stir to combine.
4. Reduce the heat to medium. Add the stir-fry sauce, and mix well. Cook for about 5 minutes, or until the cabbage is slightly wilted but still a bit crunchy. The sauce should be bubbling. Remove from the heat. Transfer to a serving bowl.
5. Sprinkle with the scallions and sesame seeds before serving.

❋ **SUBSTITUTION TIP:** Try ground pork instead of chicken to make a more traditional egg roll filling.

Per Serving: Calories: 262; Total fat: 9g; Saturated fat: 1g; Protein: 29g; Carbs: 17g; Sugar: 10g; Fiber: 4g; Sodium: 442mg

CHICKEN AND BRUSSELS SPROUTS SKILLET

SERVES: 4 **PREP TIME:** 5 minutes **COOK TIME:** 30 minutes

I like to use chicken thighs in one-pot recipes because they retain more moisture than chicken breasts. Searing the skin side until there is a little brown on the chicken helps seal in moisture and add flavor, so don't skip this step. Not a fan of Brussels sprouts? Broccoli, cauliflower, and asparagus would be great substitutes that pair nicely with the chicken.

---

4 bone-in chicken thighs, skin removed

½ teaspoon kosher salt

¼ teaspoon freshly ground black pepper

2 tablespoons extra-virgin olive oil

1 onion, cut into half-moon slices

1 pound Brussels sprouts, trimmed and halved

1 cup vegetable broth

Juice of 1 lemon

---

1. Preheat the oven to 350°F.

2. Season the chicken with the salt and pepper.

3. In a large, oven-safe skillet, heat the oil over medium-high heat.

4. Place the chicken in the skillet so that the side that had skin faces the bottom, and sear for 3 to 5 minutes, or until browned.

5. Flip the chicken. Scatter the onion and Brussels sprouts around the chicken, and add the broth. Bring to a simmer. Remove from the heat.

6. Transfer the skillet to the oven, and bake for 20 minutes, or until the chicken has cooked through. Remove from the oven.

7. Sprinkle the lemon juice over the top of the chicken and Brussels sprouts, and serve.

VARIATION TIP: Adding a fresh sprig of rosemary to the skillet along with the vegetable broth gives this dish more flavor.

Per Serving: Calories: 259; Total fat: 12g; Saturated fat: 2g; Protein: 26g; Carbs: 14g; Sugar: 4g; Fiber: 5g; Sodium: 428mg

CHICKEN AND SNOW PEA SKILLET

SERVES: 4   **PREP TIME:** 10 minutes   **COOK TIME:** 15 minutes

In this one-skillet recipe, crunchy snow peas and carrot are combined with tender chicken pieces to make a speedy dinner you'd be willing whip up even after a long workday. You can also use chicken thighs here if you don't have breasts or tenders. Serve over rice or noodles if desired.

---

1 pound boneless chicken breast or tenderloins, cut into 1-inch pieces

1 tablespoon all-purpose flour

Kosher salt

Freshly ground black pepper

2 tablespoons extra-virgin olive oil

2 garlic cloves, minced

1½ cups snow peas, cut into 1-inch pieces

½ cup finely diced carrot

---

1. In a medium mixing bowl, toss together the chicken, flour, and a sprinkle of salt and pepper until the chicken is thoroughly coated.

2. In a large skillet, heat the oil over medium heat.

3. Add the chicken, and cook for 3 to 4 minutes, or until opaque on all sides.

4. Add the garlic, and stir to combine. Cook for 1 minute, or until fragrant.

5. Add the snow peas and carrot. Stir well. Cover, and cook, stirring once, for 10 minutes.

6. Uncover, and stir. Taste, and season with salt and pepper. Remove from the heat. Serve.

VARIATION TIP: Other vegetables, such as shallots and asparagus, are delicious in this recipe as well.

Per Serving: Calories: 221; Total fat: 10g; Saturated fat: 2g; Protein: 27g; Carbs: 5g; Sugar: 2g; Fiber: 1g; Sodium: 101mg

HOT HONEY AND GARLIC-GLAZED DRUMSTICKS

SERVES: 6   **PREP TIME:** 10 minutes   **COOK TIME:** 45 minutes

Basted with a sweet and spicy glaze made of honey, sriracha, and soy sauce, these succulent drumsticks are finger-lickin' good. Place the drumsticks under the broiler for a couple minutes at the end of baking to brown the skins and caramelize the glaze.

---

2 pounds (about 6) chicken drumsticks

1 tablespoon vegetable oil

½ teaspoon kosher salt

½ teaspoon freshly ground black pepper

½ cup honey

2 tablespoons sriracha or other hot sauce

2 tablespoons soy sauce

2 garlic cloves, minced

---

1. Preheat the oven to 425°F. Line a rimmed sheet pan with aluminum foil.

2. Using paper towels, pat the chicken dry. Brush on all sides with the oil. Season evenly with the salt and pepper.

3. Arrange the chicken on the prepared sheet pan.

4. Transfer the sheet pan to the oven, and bake for 30 minutes, or until an instant-read thermometer inserted into the thickest part of the chicken reads 165°F. Remove from the oven, leaving the oven on.

5. While the chicken bakes, to make the sauce, in a small saucepan, combine the honey, sriracha, soy sauce, and garlic. Bring to a boil over medium heat.

6. Reduce the heat to low. Simmer, stirring occasionally, for 5 to 6 minutes, or until the mixture has slightly thickened. Remove from the heat.

7. Reduce the oven temperature to 400°F.

8. Baste the chicken with half of the sauce.

9. Return the sheet pan to the oven, and bake for 8 to 10 minutes.

10. To get a crispy glaze, set the oven to broil, baste the drumsticks again with some of the pan drippings, and broil for 2 minutes. Remove from the oven. Serve immediately with the remaining sauce.

VARIATION TIP: Make this recipe with 3 pounds chicken wings instead of drumsticks, and follow the same cooking instructions.

Per Serving: Calories: 355; Total fat: 16g; Saturated fat: 4g; Protein: 28g; Carbs: 24g; Sugar: 22g; Fiber: 0g; Sodium: 579mg

SEASONED TURKEY CUTLETS

SERVES: 4   **PREP TIME:** 5 minutes   **COOK TIME:** 25 minutes

This recipe proves that turkey isn't just for Thanksgiving. For this dish, turkey breast cutlets are seasoned with garlic, thyme, and rosemary and baked in the oven until fork tender. Complete the meal with a side of steamed broccoli or Roasted Cauliflower and Tomatoes (page 177).

2 tablespoons mayonnaise
1 garlic clove, minced
1 teaspoon dried thyme

1 teaspoon dried rosemary
1 teaspoon kosher salt

4 turkey breast cutlets (about
1 pound total)

1. Preheat the oven to 375°F.

2. In a small mixing bowl, stir together the mayonnaise, garlic, thyme, rosemary, and salt.

3. Arrange the turkey cutlets on a nonstick sheet pan.

4. Spread the mayonnaise mixture onto the turkey.

5. Transfer the sheet pan to the oven, and bake for 20 to 25 minutes, or until the turkey is cooked through and golden brown. Remove from the oven. Serve.

VARIATION TIP: Top with panko bread crumbs before baking for a crispy-top version of this dish. Use gluten-free bread crumbs if needed.

Per Serving: Calories: 178; Total fat: 8g; Saturated fat: 1g; Protein: 27g; Carbs: 0g; Sugar: 0g; Fiber: 0g; Sodium: 609mg

CIDER-BARBECUED TURKEY LEGS

(OP)

SERVES: 4 **PREP TIME:** 5 minutes **COOK TIME:** about 2 hours

Reminiscent of the delicious turkey legs you get at the county fairs, this version is baked until the meat almost falls off the bone and is basted in a sweet cider barbecue sauce. I like to use a smoky, tomato-based barbecue sauce in this recipe. If you like more heat, add a dash of hot sauce to the cooking liquid.

---

4 turkey legs
Kosher salt
Freshly ground black pepper

1 to 2 tablespoons extra-virgin olive oil

1 cup barbecue sauce
1 cup apple cider

---

1. Preheat the oven to 325°F.

2. Season the turkey legs with salt and pepper.

3. In a Dutch oven, heat enough oil to coat the bottom over medium-high heat.

4. Add the turkey legs, and brown on all sides. This should take 7 to 8 minutes total.

5. Pour the barbecue sauce over the turkey, then the apple cider. Remove from the heat.

6. Cover the pot. Transfer to the oven, and bake for 1 hour. Uncover, and bake for 30 to 45 more minutes, or until the turkey legs are tender and the sauce thickens. Baste with the barbecue sauce every 10 minutes. Remove from the oven. Transfer the turkey legs to a serving platter, and serve with sauce from the pot.

 VARIATION TIP: Most grocery stores will sell turkey legs in packages of two. Try to get smaller ones so all the legs will fit in your Dutch oven. You can also substitute turkey thighs if you prefer.

Per Serving: Calories: 769; Total fat: 31g; Saturated fat: 9g; Protein: 81g; Carbs: 36g; Sugar: 30g; Fiber: 1g; Sodium: 912mg

TURKEY AND BLACK BEAN CHILI

SERVES: 6   **PREP TIME:** 5 minutes   **COOK TIME:** 35 minutes

Chili is one of those stick-to-your-bones meals I turn to time and time again to feed my family. Keep a freezer stash of ground turkey and a pantry always stocked with cans of tomatoes, beans, and chicken broth, and you can easily throw together this meal with little planning. It never hurts to have a side of corn bread, too.

1 tablespoon extra-virgin olive oil	1 cup water, plus more as needed	1 (14-ounce) can black beans, drained and rinsed
1 small onion, diced	1 (14-ounce) can diced tomatoes with green chiles	Kosher salt
1 pound ground turkey		Freshly ground black pepper
1 tablespoon chili powder, plus more as needed		

1. In a Dutch oven, heat the oil over medium-high heat.

2. Add the onion, and sauté for 5 minutes, or until translucent.

3. Add the turkey and chili powder. Cook, breaking up the meat using a wooden spoon, for 5 minutes, or until the turkey has browned.

4. Add the water, tomatoes, and beans. Bring to a boil.

5. Reduce the heat to a simmer. Cover the Dutch oven, and cook for 10 minutes. Uncover, and simmer, stirring occasionally, for about 10 more minutes, or until the chili reaches the thickness you prefer. Remove from the heat. Season with salt and pepper. Add extra chili powder if you desire.

6. Ladle the chili into bowls. Serve with any additional toppings you want (see variation tip).

✳ VARIATION TIP: You can serve this chili with extra toppings—such as shredded Cheddar cheese, sour cream, and hot sauce—on the side.

Per Serving: Calories: 208; Total fat: 9g; Saturated fat: 2g; Protein: 19g; Carbs: 14g; Sugar: 1g; Fiber: 4g; Sodium: 357mg

➡️ SPICY SHRIMP
WITH VEGETABLES

P. 134

8

SEAFOOD

SPICY SHRIMP WITH VEGETABLES

SERVES: 4 **PREP TIME:** 10 minutes, plus 30 minutes to marinate **COOK TIME:** 20 minutes

Cajun or Creole seasoning is a spicy mixture of garlic powder, dried thyme, cayenne, and other herbs and spices (see tip on making your own blend). This seasoning and shrimp are a match made in heaven. Serve with lemon wedges on the side, and add any leftovers to your favorite cooked pasta for lunch the next day.

---

1 cup extra-virgin olive oil

¼ cup Cajun or Creole seasoning

¼ cup chopped fresh parsley

2 tablespoons honey

Pinch kosher salt

1 pound large (21/25 count per pound) shrimp, peeled and deveined

2 pounds mixed vegetables, such as broccoli, zucchini, and squash, diced

---

1. In a large bowl, combine the oil, Cajun seasoning, parsley, honey, and salt. Transfer half of the mixture to another large bowl.

2. Add the shrimp to one bowl, and toss to coat. Refrigerate for 30 minutes.

3. Preheat the oven to 450°F.

4. Add the vegetables to the other bowl, and toss to combine.

5. Spread the vegetables out in a single layer on one side of a sheet pan.

6. Transfer the sheet pan to the oven, and bake for 12 to 15 minutes.

7. Add the shrimp to the other side of the sheet pan, and bake for 5 minutes, or until the shrimp are just opaque and the vegetables are tender and golden around the edges. Remove from the oven. Serve.

PREP TIP: To make your own Cajun seasoning blend, in a small bowl, combine 1 tablespoon paprika, 2 teaspoons garlic powder, 1 teaspoon onion powder, 1 teaspoon freshly ground black pepper, 1 teaspoon ground white pepper, 1 teaspoon dried oregano, ½ teaspoon dried thyme, and ½ teaspoon cayenne until evenly blended.

Per Serving: Calories: 499; Total fat: 29g; Saturated fat: 4g; Protein: 23g; Carbs: 36g; Sugar: 4g; Fiber: 9g; Sodium: 789mg

GARLIC-CILANTRO SHRIMP

SERVES: 4 **PREP TIME:** 20 minutes **COOK TIME:** 10 minutes

I'm happy to eat shrimp in just about any form: in tacos, on the grill, on salads, and in the skillet, as in this recipe. We always have frozen shrimp in the freezer because it defrosts in minutes. They come in handy when my meal planning doesn't exactly go according to plan. With succulent shrimp cooked completely in one skillet, this recipe is a lifesaver! You'll love the vibrant, zesty sauce reminiscent of the classic chimichurri.

⅓ cup freshly squeezed
  lemon juice
4 garlic cloves
1 cup fresh cilantro leaves

½ teaspoon ground coriander
3 tablespoons extra-virgin
  olive oil
1 teaspoon kosher salt

1½ pounds large (21/25 count
  per pound) shrimp, peeled
  and deveined

1. To make the marinade, put the lemon juice, garlic, cilantro, coriander, oil, and salt in a food processor. Pulse 10 times.

2. Put the shrimp in a bowl or plastic zip-top bag, and pour in the marinade. Let sit for 15 minutes.

3. Preheat a skillet over high heat.

4. Put the shrimp and marinade in the skillet. Cook for 3 minutes per side. Remove from the heat. Serve warm.

❋ **VARIATION TIP:** Serve this dish with some buttered pasta, noodles, or rice.

Per Serving: Calories: 220; Total fat: 12g; Saturated fat: 2g; Protein: 24g; Carbs: 4g; Sugar: 1g; Fiber: 0g; Sodium: 1,145mg

SHRIMP WITH ZOODLES

SERVES: 2   **PREP TIME:** 5 minutes, plus 10 minutes to marinate   **COOK TIME:** 15 minutes

One of my favorite ways to cook shrimp is to grill them to get that great charred flavor. Jumbo shrimp works best in this recipe, though you could certainly make this with any size shrimp. If you're using shrimp on the smaller side, you can thread a few of them on presoaked bamboo skewers to make it easier and quicker to turn them without overcooking. For a stovetop cooking option, sauté the shrimp in a large skillet over medium heat for about 2 minutes per side.

- 1 pound jumbo shrimp, cleaned
- 1 tablespoon extra-virgin olive oil, plus more for the grill
- Juice of ½ lemon
- ½ cup marinara sauce
- 4 medium green zucchini, spiralized
- 1 tablespoon freshly grated parmesan cheese
- Red pepper flakes, for serving (optional)

---

1. Preheat the grill on the highest setting. Baste with olive oil if needed.
2. In a bowl, toss together the shrimp, oil, and lemon juice. Marinate for about 10 minutes.
3. Put the shrimp on the grill, and cook for 3 minutes per side. Remove from the heat.
4. In a small sauté pan or skillet, bring the marinara sauce to a boil.
5. Add the zucchini, and sauté for about 3 minutes, or until tender.
6. Sprinkle with the cheese, and toss. Remove from the heat.
7. Serve the zoodles on individual plates with the shrimp on top.

PREP TIP: Once you spiralize zucchini, you can wrap it in a paper towel and store it in the refrigerator overnight. The next day, proceed as outlined in the recipe.

VARIATION TIP: You can add oregano and basil to the sauce, if you wish, or spice it up with ¼ teaspoon garlic powder and red pepper flakes for garnish.

Per Serving: Calories: 347; Total fat: 10g; Saturated fat: 2g; Protein: 52g; Carbs: 17g; Sugar: 12g; Fiber: 5g; Sodium: 353mg

CLASSIC BLACKENED SCALLOPS

SERVES: 4   **PREP TIME:** 10 minutes   **COOK TIME:** 10 minutes

Satisfying and decadent, this scallop dish is a delight. The trick to getting a nice golden sear on the scallops is to dry them really well before cooking. Patting them dry or arranging them on a plate lined with paper towels and letting them rest for 10 minutes will help you avoid steaming them during cooking.

---

2 tablespoons hot
 smoked paprika

2 teaspoons onion powder

1 teaspoon garlic powder

1 teaspoon kosher salt

1 teaspoon dried thyme

½ teaspoon freshly ground
 black pepper

1 pound sea scallops, cleaned

2 tablespoons extra-virgin
 olive oil

---

1. In a small bowl, combine the paprika, onion powder, garlic powder, salt, thyme, and pepper.

2. Using a paper towel, pat the scallops dry. Dredge on the top and bottom in the spice mixture.

3. In a large skillet, heat the oil over medium-high heat.

4. Add the scallops, making sure they do not touch each other. Sear on both sides, turning once, for a total of about 3 minutes. Remove from the heat.

PREP TIP: Frozen scallops are also great in this dish. They are precleaned and just need to be thawed in the refrigerator overnight. If you don't buy a precleaned product from your fishmonger, it'll need to be cleaned before cooking. If you must clean your scallops, make sure you remove the side muscle—a visible flap of tissue that can be cut away easily.

Per Serving: Calories: 154; Total fat: 8g; Saturated fat: 1g; Protein: 14g; Carbs: 7g; Sugar: 0g; Fiber: 2g; Sodium: 921mg

MUSSELS WITH WHITE WINE SAUCE

SERVES: 4   **PREP TIME:** 15 minutes   **COOK TIME:** 15 minutes

Whenever I have guests over, I like to serve restaurant-quality dishes that look impressive but are secretly simple to make. This dish brings a certain je ne sais quoi to the table while being unbelievably easy to make. But your guests don't need to know that! Serve it with crusty bread—or, better yet, garlic bread.

---

2 pounds mussels

½ cup dry white wine

2 tablespoons extra-virgin olive oil

3 garlic cloves, minced

¼ cup chopped fresh parsley

---

1. Clean and prep the mussels. Remove any beards. (See tip.)

2. In a large pot, combine the mussels and wine. Bring to a boil over high heat.

3. Reduce the heat to low. Cover the pot. The mussels will release juices as they cook. Cook for 5 to 7 minutes, or until the mussels have opened. Remove from the heat. Using a slotted spoon, remove the mussels from the pot, leaving the liquid in the pot. Discard any mussels that have not opened.

4. Let the liquid rest for a couple of minutes, then leaving behind the grit and sediment, carefully pour the liquid off the top into a small bowl.

5. In a small saucepan, heat the oil over medium heat.

6. Add the garlic, and sauté for 30 seconds, or until fragrant.

7. Add the cooking liquid, and simmer for 2 to 3 minutes, or until slightly reduced. Remove from the heat.

8. Serve the mussels with the sauce poured over them.

9. Garnish with the parsley.

✳ PREP TIP: To clean the mussels, scrub them well using a brush to remove any sand or debris on the shell, then soak them in a bowl of fresh water for about 15 minutes. Rinse and soak them again until there is no more sediment at the bottom of the bowl.

Per Serving: Calories: 149; Total fat: 8g; Saturated fat: 1g; Protein: 9g; Carbs: 4g; Sugar: 0g; Fiber: 0g; Sodium: 207mg

SUN-DRIED TOMATO PESTO SNAPPER

SERVES: 4   **PREP TIME:** 5 minutes   **COOK TIME:** 15 minutes

Short on time? No sweat! This snappy fish recipe can be on your table from prep to serving in fewer than 30 minutes. And if you can't find snapper, you can use a firm white fish like sea bass or halibut—or even scallops. The sun-dried tomato pesto gives this dish a wonderful tang that complements the sweet, slightly nutty meat of the snapper.

---

1 sweet onion, cut into ¼-inch slices

4 (5-ounce) snapper fillets

Freshly ground black pepper

4 tablespoons sun-dried tomato pesto

2 tablespoons finely chopped fresh basil leaves

---

1. Preheat the oven to 400°F. Line a baking dish with parchment paper.

2. Arrange the onion slices on the bottom of the prepared baking dish.

3. Using a paper towel, pat the fillets dry. Season lightly with pepper.

4. Place the fillets on top of the onions, and spread 1 tablespoon of pesto on each fillet.

5. Transfer the baking dish to the oven, and bake for 12 to 15 minutes, or until the fillets flake easily with a fork. Remove from the oven.

6. Serve the fillets topped with the basil.

✳ PREP TIP: To make your own sun-dried tomato pesto, pulse 1 cup sun-dried tomatoes, ½ cup basil leaves, ¼ cup parmesan cheese, ¼ cup olive oil, and 4 garlic cloves in a food processor until a thick paste forms.

✳ SUBSTITUTION TIP: Regular basil pesto would be excellent as well if you prefer that flavor profile.

Per Serving: Calories: 162; Total fat: 2g; Saturated fat: 0g; Protein: 30g; Carbs: 4g; Sugar: 2g; Fiber: 1g; Sodium: 100mg

BAKED HALIBUT WITH TOMATOES

SERVES: 4   **PREP TIME:** 5 minutes   **COOK TIME:** 15 minutes

Infused with flavor, you'll love the pairing of garlicky cherry tomato sauce with this mild, sweet-tasting fish. This baked fish dish is high on the list of crave-worthy weeknight meals. It's fantastic served with pasta, rice, or zucchini noodles.

---

4 (5-ounce) pieces boneless, skin-on halibut

1 pint cherry tomatoes

3 tablespoons garlic, minced

½ cup freshly squeezed lemon juice

¼ cup extra-virgin olive oil

1 teaspoon kosher salt

---

1. Preheat the oven to 425°F.
2. Put the halibut in a large baking dish, and place the tomatoes around the halibut.
3. To make the sauce, in a small bowl, combine the garlic, lemon juice, oil, and salt.
4. Pour the sauce over the halibut and tomatoes.
5. Transfer the baking dish to the oven, and bake for 15 minutes. Remove from the oven. Serve immediately.

✳ VARIATION TIP: Add 1 teaspoon grated lemon zest and fresh chopped parsley to the sauce.

Per Serving: Calories: 278; Total fat: 16g; Saturated fat: 2g; Protein: 27g; Carbs: 7g; Sugar: 3g; Fiber: 1g; Sodium: 683mg

EASY FISH TACOS

(30) (DF) (GF) (NF) (OP)

SERVES: 4   **PREP TIME:** 5 minutes   **COOK TIME:** 20 minutes

Fish tacos are a fun meal any day of the week. They're ready in about 20 minutes and hit the spot every time. Cod, tilapia, or flounder are my go-to choices for fish tacos, but you could use any white fish fillets. It doesn't really matter if the fish is a firm variety or more flaky; you break up the cooked fish into the tacos, so perfect presentation isn't too important. Make Street Corn Salad (page 188) as a nice side dish to complement the tacos.

---

4 (4-ounce) thin white fish fillets, such as flounder or tilapia
Kosher salt
Freshly ground black pepper

1 to 2 tablespoons extra-virgin olive oil
1 (12-count) package small white corn tortillas

1 ripe avocado, pitted, peeled, and sliced
¼ red onion, thinly sliced
1 lime, cut into wedges

---

1. Season the fillets with salt and pepper.
2. In a large nonstick skillet, heat the oil over medium heat.
3. Add the fillets, taking care not to overcrowd the skillet. Cook, flipping once, for 5 to 7 minutes, or until the fillets are opaque and lightly browned in spots. Transfer to a plate. Repeat until all the fillets have been cooked. Remove from the heat.
4. Warm the tortillas according to the package directions.
5. To assemble, divide the fillets evenly among the tortillas.
6. Top each with the avocado and onion, and serve with a lime wedge.

✳ VARIATION TIP: You can use flour tortillas instead of corn tortillas if you like them better and don't need the tacos to be gluten-free. You can also serve the tacos with a variety of different salsas.

Per Serving: Calories: 307; Total fat: 14g; Saturated fat: 2g; Protein: 26g; Carbs: 23g; Sugar: 1g; Fiber: 6g; Sodium: 106mg

ROASTED TROUT AND POTATOES

SERVES: 4   **PREP TIME:** 10 minutes   **COOK TIME:** 30 minutes

Trout is one of my favorite fish to cook at home. It cooks quickly, requires only one pan, and the fish is sweet and tender. You can buy trout as whole fish that have been gutted and cleaned or as fillets. For this recipe, I prefer to use rainbow or steelhead fillets that have had their skin removed.

---

4 (5-ounce) skinless
   trout fillets

Kosher salt

Freshly ground black pepper

1 pound fingerling
   potatoes, halved

3 tablespoons extra-virgin
   olive oil, divided

½ teaspoon paprika

2 teaspoons finely chopped
   fresh dill

---

1. Preheat the oven to 400°F. Line a sheet pan with parchment paper.

2. Using paper towels, pat the fillets dry. Season with salt and pepper.

3. In a large bowl, toss together the potatoes, 2 tablespoons of oil, and the paprika. Season with salt and pepper.

4. Spread the potatoes out on the prepared sheet pan.

5. Transfer the sheet pan to the oven, and roast for about 30 minutes, or until the potatoes are golden brown and fork tender. When the potatoes have been in the oven for 20 minutes, in a large skillet, heat the remaining 1 tablespoon of oil over medium-high heat.

6. Add the fillets, and pan-sear for 4 minutes per side, or until just cooked through and golden brown. Remove from the heat. Remove the sheet pan from the oven.

7. Sprinkle the fillets with the dill, and serve with the roasted potatoes.

✱ **SUBSTITUTION TIP:** Baby potatoes (sometimes called creamers) are a good substitute for fingerling potatoes, because they are thin skinned and can be cooked quickly with no peeling required.

Per Serving: Calories: 346; Total fat: 15g; Saturated fat: 2g; Protein: 31g; Carbs: 20g; Sugar: 1g; Fiber: 2g; Sodium: 90mg

SWORDFISH IN RED SAUCE

SERVES: 4   **PREP TIME:** 5 minutes   **COOK TIME:** 25 minutes

This swordfish not only is quick to make but also is infused with the flavors of a homemade tomato sauce. If you prefer a chunkier sauce, use a combination of crushed tomatoes and canned petite diced tomatoes. Or start with whole canned tomatoes, and break them up using a wooden spoon as the sauce simmers. If you can't find swordfish, see the tip for substitutions.

---

3 tablespoons extra-virgin olive oil

½ medium onion, diced

2 tablespoons chopped fresh parsley

3 garlic cloves, halved

1 teaspoon kosher salt

1½ pounds swordfish, cut into large chunks

1 (28-ounce) can crushed tomatoes

1 cup water

---

1. In a large sauté pan, combine the oil, onion, parsley, garlic, and salt. Simmer over low heat for a few minutes, making sure the garlic does not burn.

2. Add the swordfish, and brown for several minutes per side.

3. Remove and discard the garlic pieces.

4. Add the tomatoes and water, and simmer, stirring a few times during the cooking process, for 20 minutes. Remove from the heat.

SUBSTITUTION TIP: For this recipe, you can substitute another firm white fish for the swordfish if it is mildly flavored and can hold up to the simmering process. Sea bass, cod, pollock, haddock, monkfish, and grouper are all good options.

Per Serving: Calories: 376; Total fat: 22g; Saturated fat: 4g; Protein: 35g; Carbs: 9g; Sugar: 4g; Fiber: 4g; Sodium: 921mg

HONEY-LIME-GINGER SALMON

SERVES: 4 **PREP TIME:** 5 minutes **COOK TIME:** 20 minutes

This recipe has a wonderful balance of sweet, savory, and tangy flavors. To deepen these flavors, simmer the remaining honey, lime, and ginger mixture in a small saucepan until it is reduced by half before brushing it onto the salmon for the second time. Serve the salmon with steamed vegetables and rice for a complete meal.

1 (1-pound) salmon fillet

1 tablespoon honey

1 tablespoon freshly squeezed
   lime juice

1 teaspoon freshly
   grated ginger

Kosher salt

Freshly ground black pepper

1. Preheat the oven to 400°F. Line a sheet pan with aluminum foil.

2. Put the fillet on the prepared sheet pan.

3. In a small mixing bowl, whisk together the honey, lime juice, and ginger.

4. Brush half of the mixture onto the fillet. Season with salt and pepper.

5. Transfer the sheet pan to the oven, and bake for 12 to 15 minutes, or until the fillet is just opaque. Remove from the oven, leaving the oven on.

6. Brush the fillet with the remaining honey-lime-ginger mixture.

7. Return the sheet pan to the oven, and cook for 4 to 5 minutes, or until the fillet is fork tender. Remove from the oven.

8. Cut the fillet into 4 pieces, and serve.

PREP TIP: You can use 4 (4-ounce) salmon fillets instead of a 1-pound piece of salmon without changing anything in the recipe.

Per Serving: Calories: 178; Total fat: 7g; Saturated fat: 1g; Protein: 23g; Carbs: 5g; Sugar: 4g; Fiber: 0g; Sodium: 99mg

CRISPY COCONUT SALMON

SERVES: 4　**PREP TIME:** 15 minutes　**COOK TIME:** 15 minutes

Treat your taste buds to a tropical island vacation with this coconut-crusted salmon. This dish is a little something different from your usual baked salmon. Ideally, buy your salmon on the day you plan to make this recipe to ensure freshness.

---

4 (4-ounce) boneless, skinless salmon fillets
Kosher salt
Freshly ground black pepper

½ cup coconut milk
1 cup shredded unsweetened coconut

1 tablespoon extra-virgin olive oil
1 tablespoon finely chopped fresh cilantro

---

1. Preheat the oven to 400°F. Line a sheet pan with parchment paper.
2. Using paper towels, pat the fillets dry. Lightly season with salt and pepper.
3. Pour the coconut milk into a medium bowl, and put the shredded coconut in another medium bowl.
4. Dredge the fillets in the coconut milk and then press into the shredded coconut so both sides of each piece are coated.
5. Put the fillets on the prepared sheet pan, and drizzle with the oil.
6. Transfer the sheet pan to the oven, and bake for 12 to 15 minutes, or until the topping is golden and the fillets flake easily with a fork. Remove from the oven.
7. Serve the fillets topped with the cilantro.

✳ SUBSTITUTION TIP: The coconut crust is sweet and adds a lovely, caramelized crunch to the fish, but if you don't like the flavor, simply replace the coconut milk with regular whole milk and use finely chopped pecans, cashews, hazelnuts, almonds, or macadamia nuts instead of shredded coconut.

Per Serving: Calories: 317; Total fat: 23g; Saturated fat: 5g; Protein: 24g; Carbs: 4g; Sugar: 1g; Fiber: 2g; Sodium: 97mg

SALMON BURGERS WITH DILL

SERVES: 4   **PREP TIME:** 5 minutes   **COOK TIME:** 35 minutes

Dive into these sumptuous salmon burgers, livened up with bright and aromatic dill. Bread crumbs and egg help bind the patties together. If you have trouble forming the patties, let the mixture rest for at least 5 minutes before cooking so the bread crumbs soak up plenty of moisture and keep the burgers intact in the skillet.

---

1 pound salmon fillets

½ teaspoon kosher
  salt, divided

¼ teaspoon freshly ground
  black pepper

½ cup bread crumbs

1 large egg

2 garlic cloves, minced

½ teaspoon dried dill

2 tablespoons extra-virgin
  olive oil

---

1. Preheat the oven to 400°F. Line a sheet pan with parchment paper.

2. Put the fillets on the prepared sheet pan. Season with ¼ teaspoon of salt and the pepper.

3. Transfer the sheet pan to the oven, and bake for 15 to 20 minutes, or until the fillets flake with a fork. Remove from the oven.

4. Remove the salmon flesh from the skin. Put the flesh in a bowl, and remove any bones. Discard the skin.

5. Mix in the bread crumbs, egg, garlic, dill, and remaining ¼ teaspoon of salt.

6. Form the mixture into 4 patties.

7. In a large skillet, heat the oil over medium heat.

8. Add the patties, and cook for 5 to 6 minutes, or until browned. Flip, and cook on the other side for 3 to 5 minutes. Remove from the heat.

✳ VARIATION TIP: Serve the burgers on whole-wheat buns or over a salad for a light meal.

Per Serving: Calories: 268; Total fat: 16g; Saturated fat: 2g; Protein: 25g; Carbs: 6g; Sugar: 0g; Fiber: 0g; Sodium: 408mg

GRILLED AHI TUNA

SERVES: 2   **PREP TIME:** 15 minutes   **COOK TIME:** 5 minutes

Grilled ahi tuna brings a night out at a fancy restaurant right to your kitchen. It looks really impressive for a date night in but is ready in fewer than 30 minutes. For perfectly cooked tuna, be sure to pat the fish dry so there is no excess liquid and it can pick up the maximum flavor from the marinade. If you don't have a grill, you can easily cook these steaks in an oiled cast-iron skillet over medium-high or high heat. Serve alongside a large green salad of your choice.

FOR THE MARINADE
2 tablespoons soy sauce
1 tablespoon sesame oil
1 tablespoon rice vinegar

FOR THE TUNA
2 (6-ounce) ahi tuna steaks
Sesame seeds (optional)

1. Preheat the grill on the highest setting.

2. **To make the marinade:** In a small bowl, whisk together the soy sauce, oil, and vinegar.

3. **To make the tuna:** Wash the tuna steaks, and pat dry. Put the steaks in a bowl, and pour the marinade on top. Rub on both sides to coat evenly. Leave at room temperature for about 15 minutes.

4. Put the steaks on the grill, and cook for 3 minutes on one side and 2 minutes on the other. The steaks will be seared on the outside and pink on the inside. Remove from the heat.

5. Slice the steaks thin, and sprinkle some sesame seeds on top (if using).

PREP TIP: When eating raw or seared tuna, it is important to pick the good-quality kind. When you are at the fish market or a grocery store, inquire about the origin of the fish, how fresh it is, and whether it is sushi grade.

Per Serving: Calories: 256; Total fat: 8g; Saturated fat: 1g; Protein: 42g; Carbs: 1g; Sugar: 0g; Fiber: 0g; Sodium: 856mg

BEAN AND TUNA SALAD

SERVES: 4 **PREP TIME:** 10 minutes

Ditch the mayonnaise, and serve this bean and tuna salad with lemon vinaigrette at your next backyard barbecue or picnic. A lightened-up classic is always a winner. Try to use tuna packed in oil if possible because it is more flavorful and moist. Leftovers make for a great lunch the next day.

---

2 (5-ounce) cans solid tuna packed in oil

2 (15-ounce) cans cannellini beans, drained and rinsed

½ small onion, thinly sliced

1 tablespoon chopped fresh basil leaves or parsley

2 teaspoons extra-virgin olive oil

Juice of ½ lemon

½ teaspoon kosher salt

---

1. Put the tuna and the oil it came with in a medium bowl, and break up into small pieces.

2. Add the beans, onion, basil, oil as needed (you may not need all of it), lemon juice, and salt. Mix well, and serve immediately.

VARIATION TIP: If you have olives, capers, or anchovies on hand, feel free to add them to this salad. These flavors work very well together and will take this dish to another level.

Per Serving: Calories: 279; Total fat: 5g; Saturated fat: 1g; Protein: 27g; Carbs: 31g; Sugar: 1g; Fiber: 9g; Sodium: 517mg

BALSAMIC
VINEGAR STEAK

P. 154

9

BEEF, PORK, AND LAMB

BALSAMIC VINEGAR STEAK

SERVES: 4 **PREP TIME:** 5 minutes **COOK TIME:** 10 minutes

This balsamic vinegar steak has all the rich flavors and elegance of a steak house dinner and is best served with Gratin-Style Swiss Chard (page 185) or Spicy Roasted Potatoes (page 183). If you have a cast-iron skillet, use it. Its ability to retain intense heat will help achieve that irresistibly crispy, restaurant-quality sear on the steaks.

½ cup balsamic vinegar
¼ cup extra-virgin olive oil,
   plus 1 tablespoon

1 teaspoon chopped
   fresh parsley
2 garlic cloves, minced

4 (5-ounce) boneless rib
   eye steaks
Kosher salt
Freshly ground black pepper

1. To make the marinade, in a small bowl, mix together the vinegar, ¼ cup of oil, the parsley, and garlic.
2. Brush the steaks with the marinade. Season with salt and pepper.
3. In a large skillet, heat the remaining 1 tablespoon of oil over medium heat.
4. When the oil is hot, reserving the remaining marinade, add the steaks to the skillet. Cook to your desired doneness, 3 to 4 minutes per side for medium-rare. Transfer to a plate. Cover with aluminum foil.
5. Add the leftover marinade to the hot skillet, and cook for 2 to 3 minutes, or until the marinade has reduced by half. Remove from the heat.
6. Uncover the steaks, and serve with the reduced marinade poured on top.

SUBSTITUTION TIP: Although traditionally used for beef, this same marinade can be used for thin chicken breasts.

Per Serving: Calories: 418; Total fat: 32g; Saturated fat: 12g; Protein: 27g; Carbs: 4g; Sugar: 2g; Fiber: 0g; Sodium: 115mg

SHEET PAN STEAK TACOS

SERVES: 4 **PREP TIME:** 5 minutes **COOK TIME:** 25 minutes

This shockingly easy sheet pan dinner will transform the way you make tacos. Tucked inside warm corn tortillas, bites of juicy sirloin steak contrast with sweet and tender onion and creamy avocado. Is your mouth watering yet?

---

1 red onion, halved and thinly sliced

1 tablespoon extra-virgin olive oil

Kosher salt

Freshly ground black pepper

1 pound sirloin steaks (thin-cut preferred)

1 package small corn tortillas, heated according to package directions

1 ripe avocado, pitted, peeled, and cut into chunks

---

1. Preheat the oven to 400°F.

2. Arrange the onion slices on a nonstick sheet pan, and drizzle with the oil. Season with salt and pepper.

3. Transfer the sheet pan to the oven, and roast for 10 minutes. Remove from the oven, leaving the oven on.

4. Stir the onions, then push them to the ends of the sheet pan.

5. Place the steaks in the center, not touching each other. Season on both sides with salt and pepper.

6. Return the sheet pan to the oven, and roast for 5 minutes. Flip, then roast for 5 to 10 minutes, or until the steaks reach your desired doneness. Remove from the oven.

7. Slice the steak thinly. Fill the tortillas with the steak, onion, and avocado. Serve.

> ✳ **VARIATION TIP:** You can add cheese, such as queso fresco or shredded Cheddar, to the tacos as you're assembling them.

Per Serving: Calories: 418; Total fat: 24g; Saturated fat: 7g; Protein: 27g; Carbs: 24g; Sugar: 1g; Fiber: 6g; Sodium: 107mg

SHEET PAN STEAK
TACOS

P. 155

BARBECUE BRISKET WITH FIRE-ROASTED TOMATOES AND JALAPEÑOS

(OP)

SERVES: 6 **PREP TIME:** 15 minutes **COOK TIME:** 3 hours

Slow-roasting over low heat is the key to making the most delicious brisket. Serve the brisket as a sandwich with extra barbecue sauce, or pair with sides, such as Garlic-Parsley Sweet Potato Fries (page 181) or Arugula-Watermelon Salad (page 63).

---

1 (3- to 4-pound) beef brisket
1 teaspoon kosher salt
½ teaspoon freshly ground
   black pepper

2 tablespoons extra-virgin
   olive oil
1 (14-ounce) can diced
   fire-roasted tomatoes

3 jalapeños, seeded
   and chopped
2 cups barbecue sauce
1 cup water, plus ½ cup
   as needed

---

1. Preheat the oven to 325°F.

2. Trim the brisket of fat, leaving just a thin layer. Season with the salt and pepper.

3. In a Dutch oven, heat the oil over medium-high heat. Add the brisket, and sear for 5 minutes per side, or until browned all over. Transfer to a plate.

4. Reduce the heat to medium. Add the tomatoes and jalapeños to the Dutch oven. Sauté for 5 minutes, or until the vegetables soften. Stir in the barbecue sauce and water.

5. Place the brisket, fat-side up, back in the Dutch oven. Spoon some of the sauce on top of the brisket. Remove from the heat.

6. Cover the pot. Transfer to the oven, and roast for 2½ to 3 hours, or until the meat is tender and shredable. Check the pot once during cooking, and if the sauce is getting too thick, add ½ cup of water. Remove from the oven.

7. Remove the brisket from the Dutch oven, and shred using 2 forks. Serve with the sauce from the pot.

Per Serving: Calories: 789; Total fat: 48g; Saturated fat: 17g; Protein: 43g; Carbs: 41g; Sugar: 34g; Fiber: 2g; Sodium: 932mg

EASY MARINARA MEATBALLS

SERVES: 4 **PREP TIME:** 10 minutes **COOK TIME:** 20 minutes

Saucy meatballs are a go-to comfort food. In this recipe, you'll cook the meatballs first to give them that sought-after brown crust, then simmer them in marinara sauce to meld the flavors and make sure the meatballs stay wonderfully juicy. Serve them with pasta or in sandwiches.

---

1 pound lean ground beef

¾ cup seasoned
　bread crumbs

1 large egg

1 teaspoon garlic powder

1 teaspoon kosher salt

¼ teaspoon freshly ground
　black pepper

½ tablespoon extra-virgin
　olive oil

2 cups marinara sauce

---

1. In a large mixing bowl, stir together the beef, bread crumbs, egg, garlic powder, salt, and pepper. Knead by hand to completely combine the ingredients.

2. Roll the mixture into 1-inch balls.

3. In a large skillet, heat the oil over medium heat.

4. Add the meatballs, and brown on all sides. This should take about 5 minutes total.

5. Reduce the heat to medium-low. Pour the marinara sauce over the meatballs. Cover, and simmer for 15 minutes. Remove from the heat. Serve. To freeze, store in plastic containers or zip-top freezer bags for up to 4 months. Defrost overnight in the refrigerator, and microwave for 1 to 2 minutes to reheat.

VARIATION TIP: Instead of garlic powder, try adding 1 minced garlic clove to the meatballs for a zestier flavor. Add to the skillet after the meatballs have browned, and stir for 1 minute. You can also substitute gluten-free bread crumbs if desired.

Per Serving: Calories: 318; Total fat: 15g; Saturated fat: 5g; Protein: 28g; Carbs: 17g; Sugar: 5g; Fiber: 3g; Sodium: 678mg

POTATO GNOCCHI BOLOGNESE WITH BABY SPINACH

SERVES: 4 **PREP TIME:** 5 minutes **COOK TIME:** 25 minutes

Pillowy potato gnocchi and baby spinach are simmered in a rich Bolognese sauce and cook quickly. This dish is made in one pot, which means less dishes to clean. It is excellent served with a green salad and crusty bread.

---

1 tablespoon extra-virgin
  olive oil

1 pound lean ground beef

2 cups marinara sauce

1 cup water, plus more
  as needed

1 (16-ounce) package gnocchi

2 to 3 cups chopped fresh
  baby spinach

Kosher salt

Freshly ground black pepper

Grated parmesan cheese,
  for garnish

---

1. In a Dutch oven, heat the oil over medium-high heat.

2. Add the beef, and cook, stirring using a wooden spoon to break up the meat, for a few minutes, or until browned. Pour off any extra fat.

3. Reduce the heat to low. Add the marinara sauce, cover the Dutch oven, and simmer, stirring occasionally, for 10 minutes.

4. Add the water, and return the liquid to a simmer.

5. Add the gnocchi, making sure all are immersed in the sauce, adding extra water if necessary. Cook for 5 to 8 minutes, or until the gnocchi are tender but not mushy.

6. Stir in the spinach, and cook for 1 to 2 minutes, or until wilted. The liquid will evaporate and the sauce will thicken. Season with salt and pepper. Remove from the heat.

7. Garnish with cheese just before serving.

PREP TIP: You can buy fresh gnocchi at Italian specialty stores, but grocery stores also sell vacuum-packed gnocchi in the dried pasta section. They cook quickly, making them very convenient to use in this one-pot recipe. I don't use frozen gnocchi in this recipe because they tend to get mushy in the one-pot method of cooking.

Per Serving: Calories: 413; Total fat: 22g; Saturated fat: 9g; Protein: 27g; Carbs: 26g; Sugar: 5g; Fiber: 3g; Sodium: 428mg

PORK WITH OLIVES

SERVES: 4 **PREP TIME:** 10 minutes **COOK TIME:** 25 minutes

It's hard to narrow down my favorite pork recipes, but pork tenderloin is at the top of my list. This Italian-inspired pork dish is lean, delicious, quick to make, and impressive enough to serve to guests. Although pork is the preferred meat of southern Italy, this same exact recipe is delicious using boneless, skinless chicken thighs. Add aromatics such as parsley, basil, sage, or bay leaves for more flavor.

---

1 small pork tenderloin, cut
into 1½-inch-thick rounds
½ cup flour
Kosher salt

Freshly ground black pepper
¼ cup extra-virgin olive oil
3 rosemary sprigs, stemmed
1 cup dry white wine

½ cup green olives, pitted
and halved

---

1. Gently coat the pork in the flour. Season with salt and pepper.

2. In a large sauté pan, combine the oil and rosemary. Heat over medium-high heat for a few minutes.

3. Add the pork, and brown on all sides. This should take 6 to 7 minutes total.

4. Add the wine and olives. Reduce the heat to low. Cook for 15 to 20 minutes. If the juices are drying up too quickly, reduce the heat, and add a little bit of water. A little bit of juice should remain to top the meat with before serving. Remove from the heat.

✱ PREP TIP: Cut the pork tenderloin pieces into whatever size you prefer; the smaller the pieces, the faster they will cook.

Per Serving: Calories: 268; Total fat: 13g; Saturated fat: 3g; Protein: 24g; Carbs: 8g; Sugar: 0g; Fiber: 1g; Sodium: 223mg

FRIED PORK CUTLETS

SERVES: 4   **PREP TIME:** 5 minutes, plus 15 minutes to chill   **COOK TIME:** 10 minutes

This dish is inspired by tonkatsu, a Japanese dish made with pork cutlets breaded with flour, egg, and panko bread crumbs, then fried until golden brown. It is always served with rice, shredded cabbage, and a katsu sauce. Get an extra-good crisp by double-frying the cutlets before serving. Just panfry, drain on paper towels, and panfry again.

---

4 (5-ounce) ½-inch-thick pork cutlets
Kosher salt
Freshly ground black pepper

1 cup all-purpose flour
2 large eggs
2 cups panko bread crumbs
1 tablespoon vegetable oil

½ lemon, cut into wedges (optional)
Katsu sauce, for serving

---

1. Arrange the cutlets in a single layer between 2 sheets of plastic wrap, and using a meat mallet or rolling pin, pound to ¼-inch thickness. Season both sides with salt and pepper.

2. Gather 3 small, shallow bowls. Put the flour in the first. Season with salt and pepper. In the second, using a fork, whisk the eggs. Put the panko in the third. Season with salt and pepper.

3. Lightly coat each cutlet in the flour, then in the egg, and finally in the panko, pressing the panko onto the cutlet for an even coat.

4. Put the cutlets on a sheet pan, and refrigerate for 15 minutes to help the breading adhere.

5. In a large skillet, heat the oil over medium-high heat until shimmering.

6. Add the cutlets, and cook for about 3 minutes per side, or until golden. Remove from the heat. Transfer to paper towels to drain. Lightly season with salt.

7. Serve the cutlets with the lemon wedges (if using) and katsu sauce.

✳ COOKING TIP: If you can't find katsu sauce at the grocery store or online, you can make your own by mixing ¼ cup ketchup, ¼ cup Worcestershire sauce, 2 teaspoons soy sauce, and 1 teaspoon sugar.

Per Serving: Calories: 450; Total fat: 17g; Saturated fat: 5g; Protein: 38g; Carbs: 31g; Sugar: 2g; Fiber: 2g; Sodium: 340mg

GARLIC-GINGER PORK STIR-FRY

SERVES: 4 **PREP TIME:** 10 minutes **COOK TIME:** 15 minutes

This stir-fry comes together in a flash, so be sure all the components are ready to go before you start. Use this recipe as an inspiration, and experiment with different meat and vegetable combinations. Try substituting chicken or beef for the pork. To make this gluten-free, use tamari instead of soy sauce.

---

2 tablespoons extra-virgin olive oil

1 tablespoon freshly grated ginger

4 garlic cloves, minced

1 pound boneless pork cutlets, cut into thin strips

2 cups fresh broccoli, chopped

2 tablespoons soy sauce

Steamed rice, for serving (optional)

---

1. In a large skillet, heat the oil over medium heat.
2. Add the ginger and garlic. Cook, stirring, for about 1 minute, or until fragrant.
3. Add the pork and broccoli. Cook, stirring occasionally, for 5 to 7 minutes, or until there isn't any visible pink remaining on the pork.
4. Drizzle with the soy sauce. Cook for 3 to 4 minutes, or until the broccoli is crisp tender and the amount of liquid in the skillet has reduced by about half. Remove from the heat.
5. Serve the stir-fry over rice (if using).

VARIATION TIP: You can substitute green beans for the broccoli. Chop them into bite-size pieces before adding to the skillet.

Per Serving: Calories: 236; Total fat: 11g; Saturated fat: 3g; Protein: 28g; Carbs: 5g; Sugar: 1g; Fiber: 1g; Sodium: 527mg

ROSEMARY-GARLIC PORK TENDERLOIN

SERVES: 6   **PREP TIME:** 10 minutes   **COOK TIME:** 35 minutes, plus 15 minutes to rest

Pork tenderloin is one of the leanest and healthiest cuts of pork. Dry rubs are my secret weapon for seasoning this lean cut. A mix of salt, pepper, and rosemary makes the meat moist and tender. Note: Don't cut the tenderloin all the way through! You want a place to nestle the garlic slices so they act like little umami bombs, imparting that most sublime flavor into the meat.

---

1 (1⅓- to 1½-pound) boneless pork tenderloin
2 garlic cloves, thinly sliced

1 teaspoon kosher salt
1 teaspoon dried rosemary

¼ teaspoon freshly ground black pepper

---

1. Adjust the oven rack to the center position. Place a nonstick sheet pan on it. Preheat the oven to 425°F.

2. On a cutting board, cut halfway through the tenderloin 6 times, making the portions roughly equal in thickness.

3. Press the garlic into the cuts.

4. In a small mixing bowl, stir together the salt, rosemary, and pepper.

5. Rub the mixture all over the tenderloin, including into the cuts.

6. Place the tenderloin on the hot sheet pan, and roast for 30 to 35 minutes. Remove from the oven. Let sit for 15 minutes.

7. Cut the tenderloin into thin slices, and serve.

COOKING TIP: The longer the seasoning marinates on the pork, the more flavorful the finished dish, so if you have time, let the pork rest for 30 minutes before roasting for maximum flavor.

Per Serving: Calories: 122; Total fat: 4g; Saturated fat: 1g; Protein: 21g; Carbs: 0g; Sugar: 0g; Fiber: 0g; Sodium: 440mg

HAWAIIAN-INSPIRED KALUA PULLED PORK

(NF)

SERVES: 10   **PREP TIME:** 5 minutes   **COOK TIME:** 7 hours

This is one of my all-time favorite dishes! Making this dish requires a slow and long process, but it's worth the extra time and effort. The resulting succulent, smoky pulled pork is amazing over rice, in sandwiches, in nachos, on pizzas—you name it, this pulled pork makes it shine!

---

1 (5- to 6-pound) pork butt
1 tablespoon kosher salt
½ tablespoon liquid smoke

2 tablespoons soy sauce
2 to 4 cups water

1 (12-count) package
   Hawaiian sweet rolls, such
   as King's Hawaiian

---

1. Preheat the oven to 275°F.

2. Put the pork in a roasting pan. Using a small knife, score the meat all over to create a diamond pattern.

3. Rub the salt, liquid smoke, and soy sauce onto the meat, taking care to get them into the cracks.

4. Pour 2 cups of water into the pan. Cover with aluminum foil.

5. Transfer the roasting pan to the oven, and cook for 6 to 7 hours, or until the pork is fork tender. If the liquid level in the roasting pan gets low, add more water (up to 2 more cups if necessary). Remove from the oven. Uncover, and let cool enough to be able to handle.

6. Shred the pork, and mix with the pan sauce.

7. Serve the pork tucked into the Hawaiian rolls (or anywhere else you want to put it).

PREP TIP: For even better results, line the roasting pan with banana leaves, enclosing the pork in them. Cover the pan with foil, and proceed, discarding the banana leaves before serving.

COOKING TIP: To speed up the process, cook the pork at 350°F for about 4 hours, taking care to add water to the roasting pan as needed to prevent burning.

Per Serving: Calories: 552; Total fat: 30g; Saturated fat: 10g; Protein: 43g; Carbs: 22g; Sugar: 2g; Fiber: 2g; Sodium: 1,021mg

COUNTRY-STYLE PORK RAGÙ

SERVES: 6   **PREP TIME:** 5 minutes   **COOK TIME:** 2 hours 45 minutes

Inspired by the classic Italian meat sauce, this rich and hearty pork ragù gets its vibrant flavor from garlic, red wine, and seasoned crushed tomatoes. Although not traditional, for creamy texture, try finishing it with a dollop of tangy crème fraîche, stirred in just before serving.

- 1 tablespoon extra-virgin olive oil
- 2 to 3 pounds boneless country-style pork ribs
- 1 teaspoon kosher salt, plus more for seasoning
- ½ teaspoon freshly ground black pepper, plus more for seasoning
- 3 garlic cloves, chopped
- ½ cup red wine
- 1 (28-ounce) can crushed tomatoes with basil and oregano
- Cooked pasta or rice, for serving (optional)

---

1. Preheat the oven to 325°F.
2. In a large Dutch oven, heat the oil over medium heat.
3. Season the ribs with the salt and pepper. Add to the Dutch oven, and brown for 5 minutes per side. Transfer to a large plate.
4. Add the garlic to the Dutch oven, and cook for 2 minutes, or until slightly golden.
5. Add the wine to deglaze, stirring up any browned bits from the bottom.
6. Add the tomatoes, and return the ribs to the Dutch oven. Remove from the heat.
7. Cover the pot. Transfer to the oven, and bake for 2 to 2½ hours, or until the meat is falling apart. Remove from the oven.
8. Using 2 forks, shred the meat. Discard the bones. Mix the shredded meat with the gravy. Season with salt and pepper.
9. Serve the ragù as is or over your favorite pasta or rice.

COOKING TIP: I prefer to make this a day ahead, then heat it up in my Dutch oven on the stovetop to serve it. The flavors marry overnight and are deeper and richer the next day.

Per Serving: Calories: 329; Total fat: 20g; Saturated fat: 4g; Protein: 30g; Carbs: 5g; Sugar: 3g; Fiber: 2g; Sodium: 496mg

ROASTED SAUSAGES WITH POTATOES AND PEPPERS

SERVES: 4   **PREP TIME:** 10 minutes   **COOK TIME:** 35 to 40 minutes

I'm a big fan of sheet pan dinners and for good reason: they're versatile, and cleanup is always a no-brainer. When roasted, the peppers caramelize and the sausages become crispy on the outside and juicy on the inside. This recipe is tailored to serve four people, but you can double or triple it to feed a crowd.

---

4 bell peppers of mixed colors, cored and cut into strips

6 hot pork sausages, cut into 4 pieces

4 or 5 medium potatoes, peeled and diced

¼ cup extra-virgin olive oil, plus more for the pan

½ teaspoon minced fresh rosemary leaves

1 large onion, sliced

Kosher salt

Freshly ground black pepper

---

1. Put a large roasting pan or rimmed sheet pan in the oven to heat. Preheat the oven to 400°F.

2. In a large bowl, combine the peppers, sausages, potatoes, oil, rosemary, and onion. Using clean hands or a spatula, mix all the ingredients well. Season with salt and pepper.

3. Add a few tablespoons of olive oil to the heated pan, and add all the ingredients, spreading evenly. Bake, turning the ingredients once or twice using a wooden spoon or spatula to ensure they are not sticking to the pan, for 35 to 40 minutes, or until the sausages have cooked through and the vegetables are tender. Remove from the oven. Serve.

VARIATION TIP: Mushrooms, olives, and fresh tomatoes make for great additions or substitutions in this recipe. Add more Italian herbs as desired.

Per Serving: Calories: 681; Total fat: 42g; Saturated fat: 14g; Protein: 23g; Carbs: 53g; Sugar: 3g; Fiber: 7g; Sodium: 786mg

BRAISED LAMB SHANKS

SERVES: 4 **PREP TIME:** 10 minutes **COOK TIME:** 2 hours 25 minutes

Craving something warm and hearty that'll stick to your ribs? These lamb shanks fit the bill and are sure to draw the whole family to the table. Braising turns this tough and often overlooked cut into a fall-off-the-bone-tender morsel. You'll be glad you made this recipe when it slowly fills your house with the most enticing aromas. Serve warm with rice or couscous.

3 tablespoons extra-virgin olive oil

6 lamb shanks

1 large onion, chopped

3 carrots, chopped

1 (15-ounce) can diced tomatoes

6 cups water

3 bay leaves

1 teaspoon kosher salt

1. Heat a large pot with a lid or Dutch oven over high heat.
2. Pour in the oil, and add the lamb shanks. Brown on each side. This should take about 8 minutes total. Transfer to a plate.
3. Add the onion and carrots to the Dutch oven. Cook for 5 minutes.
4. Add the tomatoes, water, bay leaves, and salt. Stir to combine.
5. Return the lamb shanks to the Dutch oven, and bring to a simmer.
6. Reduce the heat to low. Cover the Dutch oven, and cook for 1½ hours.
7. Uncover the Dutch oven, and cook for 20 minutes. Remove from the heat.
8. Remove and discard the bay leaves. Spoon the lamb shanks and sauce onto a serving dish. Serve warm.

COOKING TIP: If you want to reduce the cooking time, use a pressure cooker, and cut the cook time to 45 minutes. Or you can follow steps 1 through 5 in a pot, then transfer everything to a slow cooker and cook on low for 4 to 6 hours.

Per Serving: Calories: 452; Total fat: 30g; Saturated fat: 9g; Protein: 36g; Carbs: 12g; Sugar: 6g; Fiber: 4g; Sodium: 766mg

GREEK-STYLE LAMB BURGERS

SERVES: 4   **PREP TIME:** 10 minutes   **COOK TIME:** 10 minutes

This recipe puts a Mediterranean spin on classic cheeseburgers by stuffing feta cheese *inside* the lamb patties. Dress these gourmet Greek-style burgers with toppings, such as fresh tomato, tzatziki sauce, or olive tapenade. You'll never look at burger night the same way again.

Nonstick cooking spray, for coating the skillet (optional)

1 pound ground lamb

½ teaspoon kosher salt

½ teaspoon freshly ground black pepper

4 tablespoons feta cheese, crumbled

Buns, toppings, and tzatziki, for serving (optional)

---

1. Preheat a grill, grill pan, or skillet on high heat. (If using a skillet, lightly oil with cooking spray.)

2. In a large bowl, using your hands, combine the lamb, salt, and pepper.

3. Divide the meat into 4 portions. Divide each portion in half to make a top and a bottom. Flatten each half into a 3-inch circle.

4. Make a dent in the center of one of the halves, and place 1 tablespoon of cheese in the center. Place the second half of the patty on top of the cheese, and press down to close the 2 halves together, making it resemble a round burger. Repeat with the remaining meat and cheese.

5. Put the patties on the grill, and cook for 3 minutes per side for medium-well. Remove from the heat.

6. Serve the patties on buns with your favorite toppings and tzatziki sauce (if using).

✳ **VARIATION TIP:** You can add a teaspoon of fresh thyme or chopped rosemary to the lamb for even more great taste. You can also easily turn this into a gourmet burger with fancy toppings, like sautéed mushrooms or Dijon mustard.

Per Serving: Calories: 345; Total fat: 28g; Saturated fat: 12g; Protein: 20g; Carbs: 0g; Sugar: 0g; Fiber: 0g; Sodium: 444mg

SMOKY HERBED
LAMB CHOPS WITH
LEMON-ROSEMARY
DRESSING

P. 170

SMOKY HERBED LAMB CHOPS WITH LEMON-ROSEMARY DRESSING

SERVES: 6   **PREP TIME:** 1 hour 35 minutes   **COOK TIME:** 10 minutes

Lamb is often overlooked as an easy grilled meat in favor of chicken or steak. Marinating lamb chops before grilling gives them a ton of flavor. Don't be hesitant about cooking the lamb to medium or medium-rare. Overcooking lamb chops tends to dry them out and make them tough.

---

4 large garlic cloves

1 cup freshly squeezed
   lemon juice

⅓ cup fresh rosemary leaves

1 cup extra-virgin olive oil

1½ teaspoons kosher salt

1 teaspoon freshly ground
   black pepper

6 (1-inch-thick) lamb chops

Nonstick cooking spray, for
   coating the skillet (optional)

---

1. To make the dressing, put the garlic, lemon juice, rosemary, oil, salt, and pepper in a food processor or blender. Blend for 15 seconds.

2. Put the lamb chops in a large plastic zip-top bag or container. Cover the lamb chops with two-thirds of the dressing, making sure that all are coated. Let marinate in the refrigerator for 1 hour.

3. When you are almost ready to eat, take the lamb chops out of the refrigerator, and let sit on the countertop for 20 minutes.

4. Preheat a grill, grill pan, or skillet on high heat. (If using a skillet, lightly oil with cooking spray.)

5. Add the lamb chops, and cook for 3 minutes per side. Remove from the heat.

6. To serve, drizzle the lamb with the remaining dressing.

❋ VARIATION TIP: If you don't like rosemary, you can replace it with 1 cup fresh cilantro leaves.

Per Serving: Calories: 421; Total fat: 38g; Saturated fat: 13g; Protein: 18g; Carbs: 1g; Sugar: 0g; Fiber: 0g; Sodium: 459mg

RUSTIC POTATO
GALETTE

P. 184

10

SIDES

BRAISED GREEN BEANS
WITH TOMATOES

(30) (DF) (GF) (NF) (OP) (VG)

SERVES: 4 **PREP TIME:** 10 minutes **COOK TIME:** 20 minutes

Here's a no-fuss way to dress up fresh green beans. Braised with tomatoes, garlic, and onion until tender, these green beans require very little hands-on cooking. You won't get overwhelmed preparing this side dish while cooking everything else for dinner. Garnish with fresh chopped basil before serving, if desired.

¼ cup extra-virgin olive oil

1 large onion, chopped

4 garlic cloves, finely chopped

1 pound fresh or frozen green beans, trimmed and cut into 2-inch pieces

1½ teaspoons kosher salt, divided

1 (15-ounce) can diced tomatoes

½ teaspoon freshly ground black pepper

---

1. In a large pot, combine the oil, onion, and garlic. Cook over medium heat for 1 minute.

2. Add the green beans and 1 teaspoon of salt. Toss everything together, and cook for 3 minutes.

3. Add the diced tomatoes with their juices, remaining ½ teaspoon of salt, and the pepper. Cook, stirring occasionally, for 12 minutes. Remove from the heat. Serve warm.

✳ **VARIATION TIP:** For an added crunch, you can sprinkle toasted almonds or pine nuts on top when you are ready to serve. I also like to add ½ teaspoon red pepper flakes for a little spice and then finish it off with a generous squeeze of lemon.

Per Serving: Calories: 191; Total fat: 14g; Saturated fat: 2g; Protein: 4g; Carbs: 16g; Sugar: 8g; Fiber: 6g; Sodium: 567mg

BALSAMIC GREEN BEANS WITH SHALLOT

SERVES: 6 **PREP TIME:** 5 minutes **COOK TIME:** 30 minutes

Green beans never tasted so good. The sweet and tangy flavors of the sautéed shallot and a syrupy balsamic reduction take the common side dish to a whole new level. Serve this at your holiday table, using the acidity of the balsamic vinegar to balance out richer flavors.

1 (16-ounce) bag frozen green beans	1 tablespoon extra-virgin olive oil	¼ cup balsamic vinegar
¾ cup water	1 medium shallot, minced	Kosher salt
		Freshly ground black pepper

1. In a Dutch oven, combine the green beans and water. Cover, and bring to a boil over medium-high heat. Steam for about 5 minutes, or until tender. Drain in a colander.

2. Add the oil and shallot to the Dutch oven. Sauté over medium-high heat for a few minutes, or until soft.

3. Add the vinegar, and cook for 5 to 10 minutes, or until the liquid has reduced by half.

4. Return the beans to the Dutch oven, and toss with the vinegar and shallot. Cook, stirring, for 3 to 5 minutes, or until the beans are well coated with the sauce. Remove from the heat. Season with salt and pepper. Serve.

COOKING TIP: For even easier prep, buy green beans that can be microwaved in the bag. Follow the instructions on the bag, and you are ready for step 4.

Per Serving: Calories: 60; Total fat: 2g; Saturated fat: 0g; Protein: 1g; Carbs: 8g; Sugar: 3g; Fiber: 2g; Sodium: 31mg

GINGERY GLAZED ROASTED BRUSSELS SPROUTS WITH RED ONION

SERVES: 4   **PREP TIME:** 10 minutes   **COOK TIME:** 30 minutes

This dish is guaranteed to convert even the most resistant eater into a Brussels sprouts fan. The key is letting the Brussels sprouts roast and caramelize in the oven, giving them a crispy, sweet, and slightly burnt taste that will have your guests coming back for seconds. The gingery glaze enhances the natural sweetness of this roasted vegetable and makes for a zesty layer that you can't resist.

---

4 cups Brussels sprouts, quartered

1 small red onion

1 tablespoon vegetable oil

Kosher salt

Freshly ground black pepper

1 tablespoon soy sauce

1 tablespoon seasoned rice vinegar

1 teaspoon freshly grated ginger

---

1. Preheat the oven to 400°F.

2. Spread the Brussels sprouts out on a nonstick sheet pan.

3. Quarter the onion, then halve each quarter.

4. Spread the onion out on the sheet pan with the Brussels sprouts. Drizzle with the oil. Season liberally with salt and pepper. Toss together.

5. Transfer the sheet pan to the oven, and roast for 15 minutes. Stir, and roast for 5 more minutes. Remove from the oven, leaving the oven on.

6. To make the glaze, in a small mixing bowl, whisk together the soy sauce, vinegar, and ginger.

7. Drizzle the glaze over the Brussels sprouts, and toss to coat.

8. Return the sheet pan to the oven, and roast for 5 to 10 minutes, or until the Brussels sprouts are well glazed. Remove from the oven. Serve.

SUBSTITUTION TIP: Substitute tamari for soy sauce if you want to make this dish gluten-free.

Per Serving: Calories: 79; Total fat: 4g; Saturated fat: 0g; Protein: 4g; Carbs: 10g; Sugar: 3g; Fiber: 4g; Sodium: 281mg

ROASTED CAULIFLOWER AND TOMATOES

SERVES: 4   **PREP TIME:** 5 minutes   **COOK TIME:** 20 minutes

On our weekly grocery store runs, we always add a head or two of cauliflower to our cart. My family is happy to eat it simply steamed, but roasting it with cherry tomatoes gives this humble vegetable a distinctly sweet, tangy taste. Try garnishing this dish with chopped fresh herbs like basil or parsley to add a hit of freshness and eye-catching greenery.

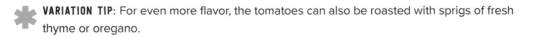

4 cups cauliflower, cut into 1-inch pieces

6 tablespoons extra-virgin olive oil, divided

1 teaspoon kosher salt, divided

4 cups cherry tomatoes

½ teaspoon freshly ground black pepper

½ cup grated parmesan cheese

1. Preheat the oven to 425°F.
2. In a large bowl, combine the cauliflower, 3 tablespoons of oil, and ½ teaspoon of salt. Toss to evenly coat.
3. Spread the cauliflower out in an even layer on a sheet pan.
4. In another large bowl, combine the tomatoes, remaining 3 tablespoons of oil, and remaining ½ teaspoon of salt. Toss to coat evenly. Transfer to another sheet pan.
5. Transfer the sheet pans to the oven, and roast for 17 to 20 minutes, or until the cauliflower has lightly browned and the tomatoes are plump. Remove from the oven.
6. Using a spatula, spoon the cauliflower into a serving dish, and top with the tomatoes, pepper, and cheese. Serve warm.

VARIATION TIP: For even more flavor, the tomatoes can also be roasted with sprigs of fresh thyme or oregano.

Per Serving: Calories: 285; Total fat: 24g; Saturated fat: 5g; Protein: 7g; Carbs: 13g; Sugar: 6g; Fiber: 3g; Sodium: 847mg

CRISPY BREADED CAULIFLOWER

SERVES: 4   **PREP TIME:** 5 minutes   **COOK TIME:** 30 minutes

These baked breaded cauliflower florets are incredible! Tender pieces of cauliflower are coated with bread crumbs, then baked until crispy and golden brown. Serve them with your favorite dip, or toss with cayenne pepper hot sauce and melted butter for a meatless version of Buffalo "wings." Bring them out during game day, and they'll be gone before the first touchdown.

Nonstick cooking spray, for coating the sheet pan

1 head cauliflower, trimmed so only the florets remain

1 teaspoon kosher salt

1¼ cups fresh bread crumbs

½ cup freshly grated parmesan cheese

2 large eggs, lightly beaten

---

1. Preheat the oven to 375°F. Spray a sheet pan with cooking spray.

2. In a medium saucepan, combine the cauliflower and salt. Cover with water, and bring to a full boil. Cook for 4 to 5 minutes. Remove from the heat. Drain in a colander, and rinse under cold water.

3. Meanwhile, in a medium bowl, mix together the bread crumbs and cheese.

4. Dredge 1 floret in the beaten egg, then coat in the bread crumb and cheese mixture. Put on the prepared sheet pan. Repeat with the remaining florets.

5. Transfer the sheet pan to the oven, and bake, turning halfway through for even cooking, for 20 minutes. Remove from the oven.

COOKING TIP: Instead of baking, you can air-fry the cauliflower florets at 350°F for 15 to 20 minutes, or until golden brown.

Per Serving: Calories: 205; Total fat: 7g; Saturated fat: 3g; Protein: 12g; Carbs: 24g; Sugar: 4g; Fiber: 4g; Sodium: 935mg

TOMATO-GARLIC
ROASTED
ASPARAGUS

P. 180

TOMATO-GARLIC ROASTED ASPARAGUS

(30) (DF) (GF) (NF) (OP) (VG)

SERVES: 4 **PREP TIME:** 5 minutes **COOK TIME:** 15 minutes

Fresh asparagus is a star on its own and doesn't need much dressing up. In fact, one of my favorite ways to cook asparagus is simply roasting it with olive oil, salt, and pepper and finishing it with fresh lemon juice. That being said, it's fun to give it an extra touch of flavor, and the combination of tomatoes and garlic is always delicious.

---

1 bunch asparagus, woody ends trimmed off

1 cup halved grape tomatoes

2 garlic cloves, minced

1 tablespoon extra-virgin olive oil

Kosher salt

Freshly ground black pepper

---

1. Preheat the oven to 400°F.

2. Cut the asparagus into 3-inch pieces. Arrange in a single layer on a nonstick sheet pan.

3. Top with the tomatoes and garlic. Drizzle with the oil. Season with salt and pepper. Toss to combine.

4. Transfer the sheet pan to the oven, and roast for 10 to 15 minutes, or until the asparagus is crisp tender. Remove from the oven. Serve.

VARIATION TIP: You can substitute a minced shallot for the garlic for a bit of a different flavor.

Per Serving: Calories: 48; Total fat: 4g; Saturated fat: 0g; Protein: 1g; Carbs: 4g; Sugar: 2g; Fiber: 2g; Sodium: 42mg

GARLIC-PARSLEY SWEET POTATO FRIES

SERVES: 4 **PREP TIME:** 15 minutes **COOK TIME:** 40 minutes

Got a craving for French fries? Give these sweet potato fries a try! Because they are baked and not fried, you can feel a bit better serving them as a base for cheese fries or alongside Salmon Burgers with Dill (page 148) or Greek-Style Lamb Burgers (page 168). Leaving the skin on the sweet potatoes gives them more texture and helps cut down on prep time as well.

---

1 pound sweet potatoes, cut into ½-inch-thick fry shapes

3 tablespoons extra-virgin olive oil, divided

1 teaspoon kosher salt, plus more for seasoning

½ teaspoon freshly ground black pepper, plus more for seasoning

1 garlic clove, minced

1 tablespoon finely chopped fresh parsley

---

1. Put a nonstick sheet pan in the oven. Preheat the oven to 425°F.

2. In a large mixing bowl, combine the sweet potatoes, 2 tablespoons of oil, the salt, and pepper. Stir vigorously to combine.

3. Carefully arrange the sweet potato in a single layer on the hot nonstick sheet pan.

4. Return the sheet pan to the oven, and roast, flipping once or twice, for 35 to 40 minutes, or until the fries are fork tender and browned. Remove from the oven.

5. In a small skillet, heat the remaining 1 tablespoon of oil over medium heat.

6. Add the garlic, and cook, stirring, for 1 minute, or until fragrant. Pour over the fries.

7. Sprinkle with the parsley, and toss well. Taste, and season with salt and pepper. Serve.

COOKING TIP: Preheating the sheet pan in the oven results in a crispier exterior for the sweet potatoes because they start cooking on contact. You can skip this step, if you prefer, and instead line the sheet pan with nonstick aluminum foil.

Per Serving: Calories: 178; Total fat: 10g; Saturated fat: 1g; Protein: 2g; Carbs: 20g; Sugar: 1g; Fiber: 3g; Sodium: 589mg

FRIED PEPPERS WITH POTATOES

SERVES: 4　**PREP TIME:** 15 minutes　**COOK TIME:** 20 minutes

In this recipe, potatoes are fried with colorful peppers and onions, resulting in parts that are crisp and brown with other parts that are tender and creamy. Waxy potatoes, like Yukon Gold and red potatoes, work best for this recipe. They have a little more moisture and are less starchy so they hold their shape well during the cooking process.

⅓ cup extra-virgin olive oil, plus more as needed

3 or 4 large bell peppers of mixed colors, cored and cut into strips

3 medium potatoes, peeled and cut into ¼-inch strips

1 medium onion, thinly sliced

1 teaspoon kosher salt

1 teaspoon dried oregano

1 tablespoon chopped fresh parsley

1. In a large skillet or sauté pan, heat the oil over medium-high heat.

2. Add the peppers, potatoes, onion, salt, oregano, and parsley. Stir to combine.

3. Reduce the heat to medium. Mix all the ingredients well, making sure that the potatoes do not stick to the skillet (see tip). Adjust the heat accordingly. Fry, stirring frequently, for about 20 minutes, or until the vegetables are caramelized and tender. Add more oil as needed. Remove from the heat. Serve hot.

✳ COOKING TIP: Potatoes tend to stick, even in nonstick skillets. If you notice that they are sticking to the skillet, reduce the heat, and add a few more tablespoons of oil.

Per Serving: Calories: 331; Total fat: 18g; Saturated fat: 3g; Protein: 5g; Carbs: 38g; Sugar: 8g; Fiber: 7g; Sodium: 598mg

SPICY ROASTED POTATOES

SERVES: 4   **PREP TIME:** 20 minutes   **COOK TIME:** 25 minutes, plus 5 minutes to cool

Roasted potatoes are always a good accompaniment to meat dishes, such as Balsamic Vinegar Steak (page 154) and Braised Lamb Shanks (page 167). To bring out great flavor in roasted potatoes, embellish them with a little cayenne for some heat and cilantro for a burst of freshness. These ingredients are really all you need to create a fantastic side dish.

1½ pounds red potatoes or Yukon Gold potatoes, scrubbed, patted dry, and cut into ½-inch pieces

3 tablespoons garlic, minced

1½ teaspoons kosher salt

¼ cup extra-virgin olive oil

½ cup fresh cilantro, chopped

½ teaspoon freshly ground black pepper

¼ teaspoon cayenne

3 tablespoons freshly squeezed lemon juice

1. Preheat the oven to 450°F.

2. In a bowl, combine the potatoes, garlic, salt, and oil. Toss together to evenly coat.

3. Spread the potatoes out evenly on a sheet pan.

4. Transfer the sheet pan to the oven, and roast, turning using a spatula halfway through, for 25 minutes, or until the edges of the potatoes start to brown. Remove from the oven. Let cool for 5 minutes. Using a spatula, transfer to a bowl.

5. Add the cilantro, pepper, cayenne, and lemon juice. Toss until mixed well. Serve warm.

VARIATION TIP: Cilantro can be replaced with fresh basil or parsley.

Per Serving: Calories: 251; Total fat: 14g; Saturated fat: 2g; Protein: 4g; Carbs: 30g; Sugar: 3g; Fiber: 3g; Sodium: 905mg

RUSTIC POTATO GALETTE

SERVES: 4   **PREP TIME:** 15 minutes   **COOK TIME:** 30 minutes

There's something very satisfying about making potato galettes—you arrange layers of thinly sliced potatoes, sprinkle on cheese, and watch the layers stack up. Don't worry if your potato slices are not perfectly uniform in thickness. This rustic galette is very forgiving, so have fun with it.

---

2 tablespoons extra-virgin olive oil, plus more for coating the pie plate

1 pound Yukon Gold potatoes, scrubbed and cut into ⅛-inch-thick slices

½ cup grated Gruyère cheese

2 shallots, finely chopped

1 teaspoon minced fresh rosemary leaves

Kosher salt

Freshly ground black pepper

3 tablespoons grated parmesan cheese, divided

---

1. Preheat the oven to 450°F. Brush a 10-inch pie plate or cast-iron skillet with a little olive oil.

2. In a large bowl, combine the potatoes, Gruyère cheese, shallots, rosemary, and oil. Season with salt and pepper.

3. Arrange half of the potatoes inside the plate in concentric circles, overlapping the slices slightly.

4. Sprinkle with about 1½ tablespoons of parmesan cheese. Repeat the process once more with the remaining potatoes and 1½ tablespoons of parmesan cheese.

5. Transfer the plate to the oven, and roast for 30 minutes, or until the top is golden and the potatoes are tender. Remove from the oven. Serve.

✱ **SUBSTITUTION TIP:** Swiss cheese will work nicely in this dish in place of Gruyère.

Per Serving: Calories: 219; Total fat: 12g; Saturated fat: 4g; Protein: 7g; Carbs: 21g; Sugar: 1g; Fiber: 3g; Sodium: 160mg

GRATIN-STYLE SWISS CHARD

SERVES: 4   **PREP TIME:** 15 minutes   **COOK TIME:** 15 minutes

Next time you see Swiss chard at the farmers' market or grocery store, pick up a bunch or two, and make this recipe. Once chard is cooked, the bitterness lessens, and that sweet, earthy flavor becomes more prevalent. Look for rainbow chard for a fun, colorful spin on this recipe.

Kosher salt

2 large bunches Swiss chard, cut into 1-inch pieces

3 tablespoons extra-virgin olive oil

½ cup bread crumbs, plus 2 tablespoons

¼ cup grated parmesan cheese

1. Bring a large stockpot of salted water to a boil over high heat.
2. Add the Swiss chard, and cook for 10 minutes. Remove from the heat. Drain in a colander, and transfer to a large sauté pan.
3. Add the oil and ½ cup of bread crumbs. Cook over medium heat, mixing well, for 2 minutes. Remove from the heat.
4. Add the cheese. Mix well so the cheese melts fully.
5. Add the 2 remaining tablespoons of bread crumbs, and mix well. Serve immediately.

✳ PREP TIP: If you're prepping a large meal and want to get a head start, you can boil the Swiss chard up to 8 hours before, refrigerate it, and complete the sauté steps right before serving.

Per Serving: Calories: 156; Total fat: 12g; Saturated fat: 2g; Protein: 4g; Carbs: 8g; Sugar: 1g; Fiber: 2g; Sodium: 354mg

FAVA BEAN AND CHICKPEA STEW

SERVES: 6 **PREP TIME:** 10 minutes **COOK TIME:** 10 minutes

This plant-powered stew is inspired by ful medames, a popular Middle Eastern dish made with cooked fava beans and chickpeas and seasoned with garlic, lemon juice, and olive oil. Ful is a national dish in Egypt and commonly served out of a metal jug. It's often eaten with pita, as a dip, or with a mix of crunchy vegetables as a salad. However you choose to eat it, you'll enjoy the mix of creamy, slightly sweet fava beans with the nutty, lingering flavor of chickpeas, all rolled into one delicious, filling meal.

---

1 (16-ounce) can chickpeas, drained and rinsed

1 (15-ounce) can fava beans, drained and rinsed

3 cups water

½ cup freshly squeezed lemon juice

3 garlic cloves, peeled and minced

1 teaspoon kosher salt

3 tablespoons extra-virgin olive oil

---

1. In a 3-quart pot, combine the chickpeas, fava beans, and water. Cook over medium heat for 10 minutes. Remove from the heat. Reserve 1 cup of the cooking liquid, then drain the chickpeas and beans in a colander. Transfer to a bowl.

2. In another bowl, mix together the reserved liquid, lemon juice, garlic, and salt.

3. Add the mixture to the chickpeas and beans. Using a potato masher, mash about half of the chickpeas and beans. Stir the mixture one more time to make sure the beans are evenly mixed.

4. Drizzle the oil on top, and serve warm or cold.

VARIATION TIP: Try adding more color and spice to this recipe by finishing it off with a sprinkle of cayenne and fresh chopped parsley.

Per Serving: Calories: 248; Total fat: 8g; Saturated fat: 1g; Protein: 10g; Carbs: 35g; Sugar: 3g; Fiber: 9g; Sodium: 450mg

ORANGE-KISSED CARROTS

SERVES: 8   **PREP TIME:** 5 minutes   **COOK TIME:** 15 minutes

Having baby carrots on hand is a big time-saver because they are peeled, cut to the right size, and ready to be used in a dish. This recipe for citrusy glazed baby carrots provides a side dish that stands a good chance of winning over selective eaters. The sweetness of orange and honey goes well with rich stews, like Braised Lamb Shanks (page 167).

½ teaspoon kosher salt, plus
   more for seasoning

1 pound baby carrots

2 tablespoons unsalted butter

2 tablespoons honey

Grated zest and juice of
   1 orange

Freshly ground black pepper

1 teaspoon fresh thyme
   leaves (optional)

---

1. Bring a pot of salted water to a boil over medium-high heat.

2. Add the carrots and ½ teaspoon of salt. (Note: If the water does not cover the carrots, add more, and return to a boil.) Cook for 5 to 6 minutes, or until tender. Drain the carrots in a colander, and return to the pot.

3. Add the butter, honey, and orange juice. Cook over medium-high heat for about 5 minutes, or until carrots are glazed and the liquid is reduced. Remove from the heat. Season with salt and pepper.

4. Garnish with the orange zest and thyme (if using).

VARIATION TIP: Garnish with toasted pumpkin seeds (pepitas) for extra crunch.

Per Serving: Calories: 69; Total fat: 3g; Saturated fat: 2g; Protein: 1g; Carbs: 11g; Sugar: 8g; Fiber: 2g; Sodium: 185mg

STREET CORN SALAD

SERVES: 6   **PREP TIME:** 10 minutes   **COOK TIME:** 35 minutes

Although fresh corn at its prime doesn't need much embellishment, this easy preparation really takes a plain corn on the cob to a whole new level of deliciousness. This street corn salad has all the flavors of elote—grilled Mexican corn on the cob seasoned with mayonnaise, spices, and cheese. For a traditional version, use a Mexican-style cheese like Cotija or queso fresco.

6 ears fresh corn

2½ tablespoons olive oil mayonnaise

½ teaspoon kosher salt

½ teaspoon freshly ground black pepper

½ teaspoon chili powder

¼ cup freshly squeezed lime juice

⅔ cup crumbled feta cheese

3 scallions, both white and green parts, sliced (optional)

1. Preheat the oven to 400°F. Line a rimmed sheet pan with aluminum foil, shiny-side up.

2. Put the corn on the prepared sheet pan. Brush all sides evenly with the mayonnaise. Season with the salt, pepper, and chili powder.

3. Transfer the sheet pan to the oven, and bake, turning the corn every 10 minutes, for 30 to 35 minutes, or until tender and slightly charred. Remove from the oven.

4. Cut the kernels off the cobs into a large bowl.

5. Add the lime juice, cheese, and scallions (if using). Toss gently. Season with more salt and pepper if desired. Chill until ready to serve.

SUBSTITUTION TIP: If fresh corn is not available, use 3 cups frozen corn kernels instead.

Per Serving: Calories: 195; Total fat: 8g; Saturated fat: 3g; Protein: 7g; Carbs: 29g; Sugar: 6g; Fiber: 4g; Sodium: 427mg

ROASTED VEGETABLE MEDLEY WITH BROWN BUTTER AND GARLIC

SERVES: 6 **PREP TIME:** 10 minutes **COOK TIME:** 35 minutes

Brown butter is a magic ingredient that adds a rich and nutty flavor to sweet and savory dishes like cookies, frosting, seafood, and pasta. In this recipe, tossing a medley of vegetables in garlicky brown butter takes a simple dish to a whole new level. Because it takes just a few minutes for butter to go from perfectly brown to burnt, be sure to keep a close eye on it as it cooks.

4 tablespoons (½ stick) unsalted butter

4 garlic cloves, minced

2 large carrots, cut into 1-inch pieces

3 cups Brussels sprouts, trimmed and halved

3 cups broccoli florets

1 teaspoon kosher salt

½ teaspoon freshly ground black pepper

1. Preheat the oven to 400°F.

2. In a Dutch oven, combine the butter and garlic. Cook over low heat for 4 to 5 minutes, or until the butter has lightly browned and the garlic is golden. Make sure not to burn the garlic.

3. Add the carrots, Brussels sprouts, and broccoli. Season with the salt and pepper. Toss well so everything is coated. Remove from the heat.

4. Transfer the pot to the oven, and roast for 30 minutes, or until the vegetables are tender to your liking. Remove from the oven. Serve hot.

VARIATION TIP: You can easily use different fresh vegetables in this dish. Try swapping out the broccoli for cauliflower or using 2 cups diced butternut squash instead of the carrots.

Per Serving: Calories: 115; Total fat: 8g; Saturated fat: 5g; Protein: 3g; Carbs: 10g; Sugar: 3g; Fiber: 4g; Sodium: 432mg

GOAT CHEESE-
STUFFED PEARS
WITH HAZELNUTS

P. 193

11

DESSERTS

CREAMY PEACH ICE POPS

SERVES: 8 **PREP TIME:** 10 minutes, plus 5 hours to freeze

When peaches are plump, sweet, and in season, I like to make these creamy peach ice pops to help us keep cool. I prefer the standard larger molds, which hold six to eight ⅓-cup portions. If you have extra mix left, just pour it into an ice cube tray for a smaller treat.

1 (14-ounce) can light coconut milk	**2 peaches, pitted, peeled, and coarsely chopped**	**¼ cup honey** **Pinch ground cinnamon**

1. Put the coconut milk, peaches, honey, and cinnamon in a blender. Blend until smooth.

2. Pour the mixture into ice pop molds, and freeze for about 5 hours. Store in the freezer with plastic wrap over the open tops of the molds for up to a week.

VARIATION TIP: You can create varieties of wonderful flavors by swapping out the peaches for other ingredients—you'll need about 3 cups total. Try plums, berries, mango, pineapple, and papaya in any combination or alone. Adjust the amount of honey depending on the sweetness of the base ingredient.

Per Serving: Calories: 103; Total fat: 6g; Saturated fat: 5g; Protein: 1g; Carbs: 13g; Sugar: 12g; Fiber: 1g; Sodium: 5mg

GOAT CHEESE-STUFFED PEARS WITH HAZELNUTS

SERVES: 4   **PREP TIME:** 10 minutes   **COOK TIME:** 20 minutes

Sweet juicy pears stuffed with goat cheese, honey, and hazelnut—what a treat! These gorgeous pears make for a beautiful plated dessert during the fall and would be fantastic served at a holiday party. Try them with a riesling or sparkling dessert wine to complement the bountiful flavors.

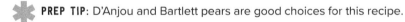

1 tablespoon unsalted butter

2 ripe pears, cored and hollowed out using a spoon

½ cup water

½ cup goat cheese

2 tablespoons honey

¼ cup coarsely chopped hazelnuts

1. Preheat the oven to 350°F.

2. In a medium skillet, melt the butter over medium heat.

3. Place the pears, skin-side up, in the skillet, and lightly brown. This should take about 2 minutes. Remove from the heat.

4. Place the pears, hollow-side up, in an 8-by-8-inch square baking dish, and taking care not to get any in the hollow part of the pears, pour the water into the baking dish.

5. Transfer the baking dish to the oven, and roast for about 10 minutes, or until the pears have softened. Remove from the oven, leaving the oven on.

6. In a small bowl, stir together the goat cheese, honey, and hazelnuts.

7. Evenly divide the goat cheese mixture among the pear halves.

8. Return the sheet pan to the oven, and bake for 5 minutes. Remove from the oven. Serve warm.

❋ PREP TIP: D'Anjou and Bartlett pears are good choices for this recipe.

Per Serving: Calories: 191; Total fat: 10g; Saturated fat: 4g; Protein: 4g; Carbs: 23g; Sugar: 17g; Fiber: 4g; Sodium: 67mg

FLOURLESS DARK CHOCOLATE CAKE

SERVES: 12   **PREP TIME:** 10 minutes   **COOK TIME:** 50 minutes

A classic chocolatey confection for any occasion, this heavenly dessert will make chocolate lovers more than happy. Don't miss out on the chance to add coffee (see tip) to enhance the chocolate flavors. Top the cake with some powdered sugar and berries, whipped cream, or both, or just enjoy as is.

---

1 cup (2 sticks) salted butter, cut into 1-inch cubes, plus more for greasing the pan

½ cup water

¾ cup coconut sugar or granulated sugar

⅛ teaspoon sea salt

1¼ pounds bittersweet chocolate (containing at least 60 percent cacao), coarsely chopped

7 large eggs

2 teaspoons pure vanilla extract

---

1. Preheat the oven to 300°F. Grease a 9-inch round springform pan, and set the pan on a piece of aluminum foil. Fold the foil up the outside of the pan, forming a waterproof layer.

2. In a small saucepan, combine the water, sugar, and salt. Heat over medium-high heat, stirring until the sugar has completely dissolved. Remove from the heat.

3. Meanwhile, bring a medium saucepan of water to a simmer.

4. Place a large bowl over the saucepan, making sure the water does not touch the bottom, and put the chocolate in it. Stir until the chocolate has melted. Remove the bowl from the heat.

5. Bring the medium saucepan of water to a boil over high heat.

6. Meanwhile, to make the batter, using a handheld electric mixer, beat in the butter 1 cube at a time on medium speed for about 2 minutes, or until well blended.

7. Beat in the sugar mixture, then the eggs one at a time.

8. Add the vanilla, and beat for 10 seconds, or until smooth. Turn off the mixer.

9. Pour the batter into the prepared springform pan, and place the pan into a larger pan. Pour boiling water (from the medium saucepan) into the larger pan until it reaches 1 inch up the sides of the springform pan.

10. Transfer the pans to the oven, and bake for about 45 minutes, or until the edges of the cake are firm. Remove from the oven. Let cool on a rack.

11. Chill the cake in the refrigerator overnight. Remove from the springform pan when ready to serve.

VARIATION TIP: Chocolate and coffee are a popular pairing because the bitterness and sweetness create an incredible richness. Stir 1 tablespoon espresso powder into the water in step 2 along with the sugar and salt. Then follow the remaining steps as written.

Per Serving: Calories: 501; Total fat: 36g; Saturated fat: 21g; Protein: 7g; Carbs: 38g; Sugar: 30g; Fiber: 4g; Sodium: 194mg

NO-CHURN STRAWBERRY ICE CREAM

SERVES: 6   **PREP TIME:** 5 minutes   **COOK TIME:** 20 minutes, plus 9 to 9½ hours to chill

Summer calls for all the ice cream, and this easy strawberry ice cream satisfies that near-daily craving. The best part is that it doesn't require an ice cream machine or continuous stirring. Fair warning though, once you learn how to make homemade ice cream, you're pretty much going to want to make it all the time—a great problem to have, in my opinion.

---

1 (16-ounce) container fresh
   strawberries, chopped
¼ cup sugar

Juice of 1 lemon
3 cups heavy cream

1 (14-ounce) can sweetened
   condensed milk

---

1. Put the strawberries in a food processor or blender, and puree. Transfer to a medium saucepan.

2. Stir in the sugar and lemon juice. Bring to a boil over medium-high heat, about 5 minutes.

3. Reduce the heat to medium-low. Simmer for about 15 minutes, or until the mixture has slightly reduced. Remove from the heat. Transfer to a large bowl. Refrigerate for 1 to 1½ hours, or until chilled.

4. Pour the cream into a large mixing bowl (or the bowl of a stand mixer). Using a hand-held electric mixer (or a stand mixer), beat the cream on high speed for 1 to 2 minutes, or just until stiff peaks form. Turn off the mixer.

5. Fold in the condensed milk until combined.

6. Fold in the chilled strawberry mixture until well blended. Transfer to a 9-by-5-inch loaf pan.

7. Firmly press a piece of plastic wrap directly against the surface of the ice cream to prevent the formation of ice crystals. Then wrap the entire pan in plastic wrap. Freeze for at least 8 hours, or until firm.

✳ VARIATION TIP: You can make this ice cream with a variety of different fruits, such as peaches, other berries, cherries, or mango. Also experiment with adding chopped nuts (walnuts would be delicious in the strawberry version) or chocolate chips.

Per Serving: Calories: 681; Total fat: 50g; Saturated fat: 31g; Protein: 8g; Carbs: 54g; Sugar: 51g; Fiber: 2g; Sodium: 130mg

COCONUT RICE PUDDING WITH MANGOS

SERVES: 6 **PREP TIME:** 5 minutes **COOK TIME:** 25 minutes

One of my husband's favorite desserts is Thai mango sticky rice, and this sweet rice pudding topped with juicy mango slices in a creamy coconut milk base is a nod to that popular dish. Garnish with toasted coconut for extra flavor and texture if desired.

---

2 (13½-ounce) cans full-fat coconut milk, divided

⅓ cup water

¾ cup dry Arborio rice

¼ cup sugar

1 (14-ounce) can sweetened condensed milk

½ cup heavy cream (optional)

3 or 4 ripe mangos, peeled and sliced

---

1. In a medium saucepan, bring 1½ cups of coconut milk and the water to a boil over medium-high heat.

2. Stir in the rice, and boil for 1 to 2 minutes.

3. Reduce the heat to medium-low. Simmer, stirring often, for 8 to 10 minutes, or until the rice has absorbed the liquid.

4. Meanwhile, in a separate medium saucepan, heat the remaining coconut milk and the sugar over medium heat for about 5 minutes, or until warm. Remove from the heat.

5. Once the rice has absorbed the liquid, add the coconut milk–sugar mixture and condensed milk. Cook, stirring often, over medium-low heat for 10 to 12 minutes, or until the rice absorbs the mixture, is cooked through, and gets creamy and thick. Remove from the heat.

6. Put the cream (if using) in a small microwave-safe bowl, and microwave for 60 to 90 seconds, or until warm. Stir into the rice mixture.

7. Divide the rice pudding among serving bowls. You can serve this dish warm, at room temperature, or chilled, with mango slices on top.

❋ SUBSTITUTION TIP: Arborio rice is best for this recipe because the plump grains stay perfectly firm and chewy. If you can't find Arborio rice, short-grain sushi rice will work, too.

Per Serving: Calories: 752; Total fat: 41g; Saturated fat: 32g; Protein: 11g; Carbs: 92g; Sugar: 68g; Fiber: 3g; Sodium: 110mg

TIRAMISU

(NF) (V)

SERVES: 8 **PREP TIME:** 20 minutes, plus 2 to 3 hours to chill

Tiramisu is a classic Italian dessert made with layers of espresso-soaked ladyfingers and custard-like cream. Traditionally, this treat is prepared by creating a delicious cream using raw eggs. As some people are hesitant to consume raw eggs, this recipe replaces them with whipping cream.

2 to 3 cups sweetened freshly brewed espresso, plus 3 tablespoons	1 pound mascarpone cheese, at room temperature ⅓ to ½ cup confectioners' sugar	1 cup heavy cream 25 to 35 ladyfinger cookies (depending on the size of your tray)

1. Pour 2 to 3 cups of espresso into a bowl.

2. Put the cheese, 3 tablespoons of espresso, and the sugar in the mixing bowl of a stand mixer (or a large mixing bowl if using an electric hand mixer). Mix on medium speed for about 1 minute, or until all the ingredients are well blended.

3. Add the cream, and mix for about 2 minutes, or until all the ingredients are well blended, light, and airy. Turn off the mixer.

4. Gently and quickly soak 1 ladyfinger cookie at a time in the reserved espresso, dipping both sides. Place the ladyfinger in a large baking dish. Continue until you have a full layer of soaked ladyfingers.

5. Spoon half of the cream over the ladyfingers, spreading evenly.

6. Dip the remaining ladyfingers in the espresso, and place over the cream.

7. Spread the remaining cream evenly over the top. Refrigerate for at least 2 to 3 hours before serving.

✳ **COOKING TIP:** For a classic garnish, dust unsweetened cocoa powder on top of the tiramisu before serving.

Per Serving: Calories: 358; Total fat: 23g; Saturated fat: 13g; Protein: 9g; Carbs: 30g; Sugar: 17g; Fiber: 0g; Sodium: 265mg

RICOTTA-LEMON CHEESECAKE

SERVES: 8   PREP TIME: 10 minutes, plus 4 hours to cool   COOK TIME: 1 hour

Traditional New York–style cheesecakes are often made with cream cheese only, but this version calls for the addition of ricotta cheese to make it lighter and fluffier. This cheesecake has a refreshing taste thanks to the lemon zest, which gives it a bright, citrusy flavor. It's the perfect dessert for picnics, barbecues, or any summer gathering.

---

2 (8-ounce) packages full-fat cream cheese

1 (16-ounce) container full-fat ricotta cheese

1½ cups granulated sugar

1 tablespoon grated lemon zest

5 large eggs

Nonstick cooking spray, for coating

---

1. Preheat the oven to 350°F. Line a 9-inch springform pan with parchment paper, and spray with cooking spray. Wrap the bottom of the pan with aluminum foil.

2. To make the batter, put the cream cheese and ricotta cheese in the mixing bowl of a stand mixer (or a large mixing bowl if using an electric hand mixer). Blend together on medium speed for 1 minute.

3. Blend in the sugar and lemon zest on medium for 1 minute.

4. Blend in the eggs; drop in 1 egg at a time, blend for 10 seconds, and repeat.

5. Pour the batter into the prepared pan.

6. To make a water bath, get a baking or roasting pan larger than the cheesecake pan. Fill the roasting pan about one-third full with warm water. Put the cheesecake pan into the water bath.

7. Transfer the pans to the oven, and bake for 1 hour. Remove from the oven. Remove the cheesecake pan from the water bath, and remove the foil. Let cool for 1 hour on the countertop. Then put in the refrigerator to cool for at least 3 hours before serving.

＊ PREP TIP: You can make the cheesecake a day or two ahead of serving. To dress up the cheesecake, top with fresh berries, such as raspberries, strawberries, blueberries, or blackberries.

Per Serving: Calories: 482; Total fat: 30g; Saturated fat: 17g; Protein: 14g; Carbs: 42g; Sugar: 40g; Fiber: 0g; Sodium: 299mg

OLD-FASHIONED PEACH COBBLER

SERVES: 6 **PREP TIME**: 10 minutes, plus 30 minutes to rest **COOK TIME**: 45 to 55 minutes, plus 10 to 20 minutes to cool

Old-fashioned peach cobbler is one of my favorite summertime desserts. With a layer of sweet, juicy peaches on the bottom and a buttery biscuit-like layer on top, it's best served warm from the oven with a dollop of whipped cream. Make it with fresh, ripe peaches when they are in season, or use canned or frozen peaches and enjoy it any time of the year.

Nonstick cooking spray, for coating the Dutch oven

2 pounds (6 to 8) sliced peaches

1 cup sugar, divided

1½ cups self-rising flour

1 cup low-fat milk

8 tablespoons (1 stick) unsalted butter, melted

---

1. Preheat the oven to 350°F. Spray a Dutch oven with cooking spray.

2. In a medium bowl, combine the peaches and ½ cup of sugar. Let sit for 30 minutes.

3. In another medium bowl, combine the flour, remaining ½ cup of sugar, the milk, and butter. Mix well until a batter forms.

4. Transfer the peaches to the Dutch oven, and spoon the batter in mounds on top.

5. Transfer the pot to the oven, and bake for 45 to 55 minutes, or until the top is golden brown and the peaches are tender. Remove from the oven. Let cool for 10 to 20 minutes before serving. The cobbler can be served right out of the Dutch oven.

SUBSTITUTION TIP: If you want to make this cobbler even easier, substitute canned peaches in heavy syrup for fresh ones. Use 2 (29-ounce) cans, but make sure to discard the syrup. Skip the ½ cup sugar that goes in with the fruit, but you will still need the remaining ½ cup for the topping.

Per Serving: Calories: 451; Total fat: 16g; Saturated fat: 10g; Protein: 6g; Carbs: 73g; Sugar: 48g; Fiber: 3g; Sodium: 393mg

OLD-FASHIONED PEACH
COBBLER

P. 201

CINNAMON-PEAR CRISP

SERVES: 8 **PREP TIME**: 10 minutes **COOK TIME**: 45 minutes

This fruit crisp will surely become the choice dessert for your fall meals. It's rustic, effortless to make, and full of seasonal flavors. Preparation takes no more than 10 minutes. The rest is baking time, and for that, you will only need patience.

6 medium pears, cored and cut into ¼-inch-thick slices

4 tablespoons maple syrup, divided

1 teaspoon ground cinnamon

¾ cup rolled oats, divided

½ cup chopped walnuts

3 tablespoons extra-virgin olive oil

1. Preheat the oven to 350°F.
2. In a bowl, combine the pears, 3 tablespoons of maple syrup, and the cinnamon. Mix well.
3. Spread the pears out in an even layer in an 8-inch baking dish.
4. In a food processor or blender, process ¼ cup of oats on high speed until powdered. Transfer to a small bowl.
5. To the oat flour, add the remaining ½ cup of oats and the walnuts. Mix well.
6. Drizzle with the oil and remaining 1 tablespoon of maple syrup. Toss to coat.
7. Crumble the mixture over the top of the pears in an even layer.
8. Transfer the baking dish to the oven, and bake for 45 minutes, or until the crumble has browned. Remove from the oven.

VARIATION TIP: Add 1 teaspoon freshly grated ginger for a spicy, warm note.

SUBSTITUTION TIP: Use gluten-free oats to make this gluten-free.

Per Serving: Calories: 233; Total fat: 11g; Saturated fat: 1g; Protein: 3g; Carbs: 35g; Sugar: 19g; Fiber: 6g; Sodium: 7mg

CHAI NICE CREAM

SERVES: 4   **PREP TIME:** 10 minutes, plus 1 hour 30 minutes to freeze

Do you love the flavor of chai? The spices in this banana-based "nice" cream mimic the flavors of the classic tea. It can be scooped like dairy-based ice cream, but without all the saturated fat and refined sugars. Note that this is best eaten fresh because it will freeze solid if left in the freezer overnight.

---

4 ripe bananas, peeled and chopped into ½-inch pieces

2½ teaspoons ground cinnamon

1½ teaspoons ground ginger

1½ teaspoons ground allspice

¼ cup unsweetened vanilla-flavored plant-based milk, plus more as needed

---

1. Line a sheet pan and an 8-by-4-inch loaf pan with parchment paper.
2. Arrange the banana pieces in a single layer on the prepared sheet pan. Put in the freezer to firm up for 1 hour.
3. Once frozen, put the bananas, cinnamon, ginger, allspice, and plant-based milk in a blender. Blend for 90 seconds, or until smooth. Add more milk 1 tablespoon at a time if the consistency is too thick to blend.
4. Scoop the nice cream into the prepared loaf pan, and freeze for 30 minutes, or until firmed up. Serve cold.

PREP TIP: Use bananas that are spotted brown and overripe to get the softness and sweetness right for this recipe. Green and just-ripe bananas tend to be too firm and will not blend to a smooth consistency.

Per Serving: Calories: 119; Total fat: 1g; Saturated fat: 0g; Protein: 2g; Carbs: 30g; Sugar: 15g; Fiber: 4g; Sodium: 12mg

MELON MINI CAKES

SERVES: 6 **PREP TIME:** 20 minutes, plus 24 hours to chill

Just as pretty as a cake made with flour, this fun watermelon "cake" is a festive, fruity alternative. There are lots of options for canned coconut milk, but only a few will work in this recipe. Make sure the only ingredients are coconut and water. If it has additives, such as guar gum, it won't whip up well.

---

1 (13½-ounce) can full-fat
    coconut milk
½ cup pure maple syrup

1 large watermelon, cut in half
    and then into 2- to 3-inch-
    thick slices

1 cup fresh blueberries
2 star fruit, cut into
    star shapes

---

1. Place the can of coconut milk in the refrigerator, upside down, for at least 24 hours before you want to make the cakes, and refrigerate the maple syrup for at least 1 hour. Chill a metal mixing bowl and electric mixer whisk attachment in the freezer for 1 hour.

2. Open the can of coconut milk, reserve the can, and discard the water. You should be left with a very thick coconut cream that is solid from being cold. Scoop the cream into the chilled mixing bowl, and return the bowl to the refrigerator.

3. Wash the can, remove the label, and use it like a cookie cutter to cut out discs of watermelon.

4. To make the whipped topping, add the maple syrup to the coconut cream in the chilled mixing bowl. Using an electric mixer fitted with the chilled whisk attachment, combine the coconut cream mixture on high speed for 1 minute, or until thick and smooth. Turn off the mixer.

5. Spoon 1 tablespoon of whipped topping onto each melon disc.

6. Top with a layer of blueberries.

7. Using 3-inch bamboo skewers, stand a single piece of star fruit on top of each melon cake. (You can also lay the star fruit flat on top of the cakes if you don't have skewers.) Serve immediately, or refrigerate for up to 3 hours before serving.

SUBSTITUTION TIP: If you can't find star fruit, you can use kiwi instead to top these colorful cakes.

Per Serving: Calories: 321; Total fat: 14g; Saturated fat: 12g; Protein: 4g; Carbs: 51g; Sugar: 42g; Fiber: 2g; Sodium: 15mg

MELON MINI CAKES

P. 205

PEANUT BUTTER COOKIES

MAKES: 18 cookies **PREP TIME:** 10 minutes **COOK TIME:** 10 minutes, plus 5 minutes to cool

You can almost never go wrong with peanut butter cookies. This eggless version of the cookie is soft and chewy and doesn't compromise on peanut-packed flavor. The natural peanut butter and whole-wheat flour make them a bit more of a wholesome treat that's no less delicious than the original. The best part is that they're ready in about 20 minutes using ingredients you probably have in your pantry right now. Just sayin'.

½ cup pure maple syrup

2 tablespoons ground flaxseed

1 tablespoon hot water

1 cup whole-wheat flour

1 teaspoon baking powder

1 cup natural peanut butter

1. Preheat the oven to 375°F. Line a sheet pan with parchment paper or a silicone mat.

2. In a small bowl, combine the maple syrup, flaxseed, and water.

3. In a medium mixing bowl, combine the flour, baking powder, and peanut butter until crumbly.

4. Add the flaxseed mixture, and combine by hand to form a dough.

5. Divide and roll the dough into 18 balls, each about 1½ inches in diameter.

6. Lay the balls out on the prepared sheet pan. Using a fork, gently press the balls down, just enough to indent them.

7. Transfer the sheet pan to the oven, and bake for 7 minutes, or just until the cookies soften. Remove from the oven. Let cool on the sheet pan for 5 minutes, then transfer to a cooling rack.

COOKING TIP: These cookies continue to bake after you remove them from the oven, so resist the urge to bake until browned.

Per Serving: Calories: 135; Total fat: 8g; Saturated fat: 1g; Protein: 4g; Carbs: 14g; Sugar: 6g; Fiber: 2g; Sodium: 23mg

CRÈME BRÛLÉE

SERVES: 4   **PREP TIME:** 15 minutes, plus 2 hours to chill   **COOK TIME:** 50 minutes

Crème brûlée is a stunning dessert—with its luxuriously smooth and creamy custard and satisfyingly crunchy, caramelized sugar on top. What many don't realize is it's surprisingly simple to make, with just four ingredients.

---

2 cups heavy cream
4 large egg yolks

½ cup sugar, plus
4 tablespoons

1 teaspoon vanilla extract

---

1. Preheat the oven to 325°F.

2. In a medium pot, bring the cream to a boil. Remove from the heat.

3. In a heatproof medium bowl, whisk together the egg yolks and ½ cup of sugar until the yolks turn a pale yellow.

4. Slowly add the cream to the egg mixture, and whisk until well incorporated. Whisk in the vanilla.

5. Place a paper towel in the bottom of a roasting pan, then place 4 (6-ounce) ramekins or ceramic mugs in the pan.

6. Divide the egg mixture among the ramekins, then fill the roasting pan with hot water until it reaches halfway up the sides of the ramekins. Cover the roasting pan with aluminum foil.

7. Transfer the pan to the oven, and bake for 40 to 45 minutes, or until the custard is set but still a little wobbly in the middle. Remove from the oven.

8. Take the ramekins out of the water. Let cool slightly, then cover with plastic wrap and refrigerate for 2 hours.

9. Evenly sprinkle the top of each custard with 1 tablespoon of sugar, and use a kitchen blowtorch (see tip) to brûlée it just until the sugar has melted and browned.

COOKING TIP: You can make crème brûlée at home the traditional way, sans blowtorch. Broil the chilled custard on high until the tops begin to caramelize (watch carefully, and don't walk away!). The caramelization may not be as even as you'd like, but it will taste delicious regardless.

Per Serving: Calories: 613; Total fat: 49g; Saturated fat: 29g; Protein: 5g; Carbs: 42g; Sugar: 41g; Fiber: 0g; Sodium: 54mg

APPLE GALETTE

SERVES: 8 **PREP TIME:** 10 minutes **COOK TIME:** 25 to 35 minutes, plus 10 minutes to cool

A galette is a rustic, free-form tart that is made with a thin layer of fruit on top of a buttery crust. Instead of making a pie crust from scratch, this recipe uses puff pastry, which is convenient and always perfectly flaky and buttery. Just thaw, roll, and bake. You'll have a delicious apple treat full of the warm, cozy flavors of fall in no time.

6 cups sliced peeled Granny Smith apples

½ cup packed light brown sugar

2 tablespoons cornstarch

½ teaspoon ground cinnamon

¼ teaspoon kosher salt

1 frozen puff pastry sheet, thawed

1. Position a rack in the center of the oven. Preheat the oven to 400°F. Line a sheet pan with parchment paper.
2. In a large bowl, toss together the apples, sugar, cornstarch, cinnamon, and salt.
3. Lay the puff pastry out on the prepared sheet pan.
4. Leaving a ½-inch border around the edge, spread the apples out in an even layer over the pastry.
5. Fold the edges of the pastry up and over the apples to form the crust.
6. Transfer the sheet pan to the oven, and bake for 25 to 35 minutes, or until the crust is browned and crisp. Remove from the oven. Let cool for 10 minutes before cutting and serving.

✳ VARIATION TIP: If you want this to be dairy-free, look for a puff pastry made without butter.

Per Serving: Calories: 256; Total fat: 11g; Saturated fat: 3g; Protein: 2g; Carbs: 39g; Sugar: 22g; Fiber: 2g; Sodium: 147mg

CRISPY COCONUT BALLS

MAKES: 24 balls   **PREP TIME:** 15 minutes

If you're a fan of Rice Krispies treats, you are sure to love these crispy coconut balls. They're as much fun to make as they are to eat. Because they resemble little snowballs, I love to make a batch of these with my daughter during the winter on snow days and enjoy them in front of a warm fire.

2 cups powdered sugar, divided	1 cup peanut butter 1 cup crispy rice cereal	1 cup shredded coconut

1. Line a tray with wax paper. Bring a small pot of water to a boil over high heat. Remove from the heat.

2. Put 1 cup of sugar and the peanut butter in the mixing bowl of a stand mixer (or a large mixing bowl if using an electric hand mixer). Cream together on low speed for 1 minute. Turn off the mixer.

3. Stir in the cereal, and form into 24 (1½-inch) balls.

4. Make a paste: Put the remaining 1 cup of sugar in a small bowl. Stir in the boiled water a little at a time until the sugar is smooth and the consistency of glue.

5. Roll the balls in the powdered sugar paste, then roll in the shredded coconut until coated completely.

6. Place the balls on the prepared tray until dry, then store in an airtight container for up to 2 weeks.

COOKING TIP: Make holiday-themed coconut balls by tinting shredded coconut with red or green food coloring. To add the tint, put the shredded coconut in a resealable plastic bag with a few drops of food coloring, then seal and shake.

VARIATION TIP: Make crispy chocolate balls by dipping the balls in chocolate ganache instead of the powdered sugar paste and coconut. To make the ganache, place ½ cup chocolate chips in a small glass bowl. Heat ¼ cup heavy cream in the microwave for 20 to 30 seconds, or until hot—but not boiling—then pour it over the chocolate. Let sit for 5 minutes, then stir until smooth.

Per Serving: Calories: 111; Total fat: 7g; Saturated fat: 2g; Protein: 3g; Carbs: 12g; Sugar: 9g; Fiber: 1g; Sodium: 47mg

STRAWBERRIES AND CREAM ICEBOX CAKE

SERVES: 9   **PREP TIME:** 20 minutes, plus overnight to chill

What's not to love about a cake that doesn't use an oven? Icebox cakes have been around for decades and are basically foolproof. Add this cake, with its delightful and classic combination of strawberries and cream, to your "baking" repertoire. The ingredients are easy to keep on hand for little celebrations like a quiet birthday at home, a hard-earned promotion, or a big game well played. No matter when you serve it, this cake always makes people smile.

1 pound strawberries	**½ cup powdered sugar**	**1½ packs Graham crackers**
2 cups heavy cream	**1 teaspoon vanilla extract**	

1. Put a metal mixing bowl in the refrigerator to chill.

2. Hull and slice the strawberries, trying to keep the slices somewhat uniform in thickness.

3. Put the cream in the chilled mixing bowl. Using an electric mixer with a wire whip attachment, beat on high speed for 1 to 2 minutes, or until stiff peaks form.

4. Add the sugar and vanilla. Continue whipping until combined. Turn off the mixer.

5. Spread just enough whipped cream to cover the bottom of a 9-by-9-inch square cake pan.

6. Top with a layer of Graham crackers, breaking them into pieces if needed to cover the entire surface.

7. Add half of the whipped cream and half of the strawberries. Repeat layers, ending with strawberries on top.

8. Cover the cake with plastic wrap, and refrigerate overnight.

9. Cut the cake into squares, and serve.

COOKING TIP: The icebox cake will be easier to serve if you pop it in the freezer for 30 minutes before cutting it into squares.

Per Serving: Calories: 255; Total fat: 20g; Saturated fat: 12g; Protein: 2g; Carbs: 17g; Sugar: 11g; Fiber: 1g; Sodium: 56mg

MEASUREMENT CONVERSIONS

	US STANDARD	US STANDARD (ounces)	METRIC (approximate)
VOLUME EQUIVALENTS *(Liquid)*	2 tablespoons	1 fl. oz.	30 mL
	¼ cup	2 fl. oz.	60 mL
	½ cup	4 fl. oz.	120 mL
	1 cup	8 fl. oz.	240 mL
	1½ cups	12 fl. oz.	355 mL
	2 cups or 1 pint	16 fl. oz.	475 mL
	4 cups or 1 quart	32 fl. oz.	1 L
	1 gallon	128 fl. oz.	4 L
VOLUME EQUIVALENTS *(Dry)*	⅛ teaspoon	————	0.5 mL
	¼ teaspoon	————	1 mL
	½ teaspoon	————	2 mL
	¾ teaspoon	————	4 mL
	1 teaspoon	————	5 mL
	1 tablespoon	————	15 mL
	¼ cup	————	59 mL
	⅓ cup	————	79 mL
	½ cup	————	118 mL
	⅔ cup	————	156 mL
	¾ cup	————	177 mL
	1 cup	————	235 mL
	2 cups or 1 pint	————	475 mL
	3 cups	————	700 mL
	4 cups or 1 quart	————	1 L
	½ gallon	————	2 L
	1 gallon	————	4 L
WEIGHT EQUIVALENTS	½ ounce	————	15 g
	1 ounce	————	30 g
	2 ounces	————	60 g
	4 ounces	————	115 g
	8 ounces	————	225 g
	12 ounces	————	340 g
	16 ounces or 1 pound	————	455 g

	FAHRENHEIT (F)	CELSIUS (C) (APPROXIMATE)
OVEN TEMPERATURES	250°F	120°C
	300°F	150°C
	325°F	180°C
	375°F	190°C
	400°F	200°C
	425°F	220°C
	450°F	230°C

INDEX

ACKNOWLEDGMENTS

Creating a cookbook is a lengthy process that involves writing, rewriting, recipe testing, and perfecting. It takes so many talented people, working behind the scenes, to bring this book to fruition. To that end, thanks to the entire publishing team at Rockridge Press, including my editor Anna Pulley for working so hard to make it happen. It was a pleasure working with everyone on this project.

Thank you to my husband, James, for lending his taste buds and perspective and for always being so flexible with what we ate for dinner. I couldn't have done it without you.

And last, but certainly not least, the warmest thank you to my family, for your encouragement and support for this project and so many others.

ABOUT THE AUTHOR

 **Karen Lee Young** is a recipe developer and author of two cookbooks, *The Electric Pressure Cooker Soup Cookbook* and *The Healthy Instant Pot Cookbook*. She is also the founder of *The Tasty Bite*, a food blog featuring recipes that make cooking from scratch as simple as possible for everyone. Her work has been featured on *Huffington Post*, *Country Living*, *BuzzFeed*, *Greatist*, and many other media outlets. Originally from New York City, she now lives in Colorado with her husband and daughter. When Karen is not in the kitchen, you'll find her enjoying the outdoors, exploring different restaurants, and traveling near and far.

CPSIA information can be obtained
at www.ICGtesting.com
Printed in the USA
JSHW010135070322
23603JS00002B/6